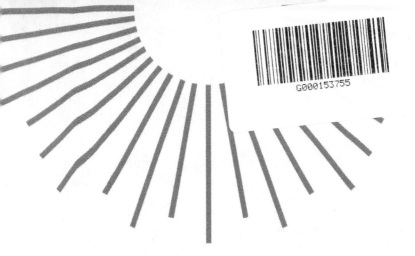

IGNITE
THE ORGANIZER
—— IN YOU ——

Discover the Life Skills You
Need to Transform Any Space

IGNITE
THE ORGANIZER
— IN YOU —

Discover the Life Skills You
Need to Transform Any Space

DANIELLE WURTH

Niche Pressworks

IGNITE THE ORGANIZER IN YOU

ISBN 978-1-946533-54-8 (paperback)

ISBN 978-1-946533-55-5 (hardback)

ISBN 978-1-946533-56-2 (ebook)

Published by Niche Pressworks; http://NichePressworks.com

Dedication

To my hubby Phil who is forever patient in listening and a committed force of love and respect in keeping our family strong while I worked on the book.

To my son Devon who offers endless hugs of encouragement when words don't need to be spoken. You are a precious gift to me when I need it most.

To my son Oliver who shows loving concern for me while working late and driving home safely. Your fun and feisty ways always make me smile.

To my sister Diana who loves me despite my endless analogies. You have supported and believed in me my whole life. Our special sisterhood is something I will forever be grateful to share with you and only you.

To my Mom who taught me to be the resilient woman I am today by being brave during times of challenge and showing me how to be my own kind of beautiful—no matter what—both within myself and in designing my home.

To my Kenny who is missed everyday but always loved hearing my client stories. I will forever cherish our porch talks and sharing sweet treats.

To my Dad and Patti who have always been my cheerleading bookends while the business grew or during setbacks. Thank you for your endless excitement and encouragement which motivated me to push forward.

CONTENTS

Matters of the Hands

MATTERS OF REFERENCE

FOREWORD

By Joe Polish

I tend to think of myself as very organized. I run a high-level marketing group, oversee a large team with thousands of clients, travel around the world, and spend a good deal of time helping to spread awareness about addiction and recovery. Most would agree that it takes an organized person to balance those many activities. Sometimes to become that organized person, it requires assistance like Danielle's.

Danielle taught me just how much more there is to organizing than I realized. She has a way of seeing solutions to problems you didn't know you had. One year, I needed to send out gifts to the 250 members of my group, called the Genius Network. Like many people, I had too many things. Danielle came up with the ingenious idea of helping me to downsize what was in my office by going through the items so that we could select which friends and colleagues I could gift significant business keepsakes. She literally got her hands dirty, sitting down with me so that we could carefully examine signifiers of my life over the past few years and analyze who I loved and who would appreciate it the most. This allowed me to connect memories to people and somehow unite tendrils of my past with my present life. Yes, Danielle manages to do the seemingly impossible—make something as mundane as organizing into a spiritual and even healing process.

As a business owner, I know firsthand how important it is to be efficient and organized. In fact, I firmly believe that without an organized space, you can't have an organized mind. My friend Tony Robbins suggests that those working with him get in the best shape of their lives. While I'm an advocate for fitness and health, I think the same is just as true for physical space: if you can't see through the chaos, both literally and emotionally, it drastically hinders your ability to become successful.

I also have a personal reason why I love Danielle's mission. As an addict in recovery, I know the importance of "cleaning house" (it's actually the fourth step of every 12-step program). What this means is taking stock of everything in your personal make-up so that you can see your relationships clearly, make amends if necessary, and move forward with a clean slate.

In this book, Danielle has managed to convey so much of what she's been able to share with me personally: specific tips and tricks for organizing a personal space as well as a deep dive into understanding the *why* behind the issue she's helping to solve. We don't suddenly find ourselves cluttering up our lives, and Danielle's life mission is to not only show us that but also show us how to escape from it.

In other words, with *Ignite the Organizer in You*, Danielle Wurth has been able to bring to the page her extraordinary gift for teaching people not only how to organize but also the emotions behind why they need to. Not everyone is lucky enough to have her nearby as a resource. But reading this book is the next best thing.

–**Joe Polish,** Founder, Genius Network
and Genius Recovery

PREFACE

I chose the word IGNITE when naming my book specifically because it conveys my mission for the reader. Each chapter will teach you how to nurture your own flame, which in turn, will permanently change how you overcome organizing challenges. Igniting your organizing flame is the first step in a chain reaction that will transform your life.

IGNITE - verb

transitive verb

1a: to set a fire: KINDLE

b: to cause (a fuel) to burn

2: to subject to fire or intense heat

3a: to heat up: EXCITE

b: to set in motion: SPARK *ignite*
a debate *intransitive verb*

1: to catch fire

2: to begin to glow[1]

---

[1]   *Merriam-Webster, s.v.* "ignite," https://www.merriam-webster.com/dictionary/ignite.

MATTERS
— OF THE —
HEART

Ignite Your Organizing Personality

Organizing is as much a *discovery* process as it is a *recovery* process.

I believe that once you *discover* an area in yourself where you are naturally organized, whether that is a hobby, work, exercise or travel, to name a few, then you can transfer those skills to a larger organizing project. Doing this will help you shift your mindset and *recover* from feeling overwhelmed and defeated in areas you might not be "naturally" gifted. The process of looking at what currently exists within you and around you and then envisioning a better future, that's the spark to flame. Once you take that newfound "spark" and gently "fan it into a flame," then BAM … a blaze develops, and you have *Ignited the Organizer in You.*

Ponder an area in your life where you are *naturally* organized. Think of a particular activity or hobby where you are independently and deeply engaged. For some people, that may be hand selecting pieces for an outfit or meticulously finding the

3

perfect materials to complete a hobby project or creating a detailed fundraising strategy for a nonprofit you support. These are areas that are important *to you* which, in turn, makes them equally important *to others*, such a spouse or family members, who wish to support you.

Just like any important project which requires support, organizing requires that same kind of common foundation for turning your home into a soothing sanctuary rather than an asylum for the insane. Instead of playing tug-of-war over muddy waters as opponents (which we all know is just messy and leads to more laundry!), you work together as a team. Just like the common mantra of marriage "study your spouse," it is ironically as important to do the same for yourself (and your family).

Let me tell you a story of how organizing led one couple from constant bickering to having a huge communication breakthrough, resulting in a more loving and peaceful marriage.

I once had the privilege of doing a consultation with an empty nester couple, Anna and Nick who wanted to transform their master bedroom. She was a former stay-at-home mom and he was a high-achieving corporate executive. Even though Anna took great care decorating their home and entertained often, Nick was frustrated that Anna filled their bedroom with endless racks of high-end quality clothing from their extensive travels.

Anna was equally frustrated that she didn't have space to properly store her fashionable clothing and accessories. This banter back and forth over the years caused constant strife in their marriage. I privately talked with Nick about his top desires for the room and then privately spoke with Anna about her needs. To my surprise they BOTH wanted the same thing … a well-organized bedroom!

Nick and Anna had failed to *discover each other's spark* that would unite them in transforming their master suite. The wife's needs were pretty straightforward: remove all clothing racks from the bedroom area, store all shoes in the closet by style and color order, hang everyday clothing that currently fit and flattered back in her main closet at an appropriate height (without the daily need for a step stool), a new hamper laundry, and an improved dry-cleaning system.

Once we *assessed* the space and its function, we *attacked* what was to stay in her current wardrobe and what was slated to go either to a nonprofit or consignment. We were ready to *assign* a solution based off the layout and accessories we discussed would work. The wife ventured off to return over $1,200 worth of blouses to one store when she realized she had an excess problem.

She called me shortly after returning the items literally gushing in excitement about her wise return and felt proud of her decision. It was a wonderful and memorable day, for we had the same plan and purpose together. This was something I had to explain to Nick. Anna's wardrobe was more than clothing. It was her hobby, and one that included many memories and travel experiences woven together.

However, my gut felt there was lost "corner piece" to their personal organizing relationship puzzle and why items were acquired in such volume. Ironically, it wasn't until our last session together while emptying a purse that held old mints and restaurant receipts dating back about eight years when a picture of their older child fell out. Anna then shared that the picture was of her daughter who had passed away.

From that day forward, their relationship began to change. Nick had a new understanding for Anna's hobby, and I noticed his anger toward the situation gradually reduced while his understanding of his wife and her choices increased.

Anna and Nick's story finally made sense to me. Anna was drawn to what mended her broken heart and overutilized that one habit for healing. Nick may or may not have wanted to acknowledge how the loss of their daughter affected his wife. As an executive, he was a man of order and wanted his home life to reflect that as well. I do believe Nick had a hard time understanding Anna and how she coped with their loss. For a long time, he couldn't accept her choices. But by working together and supporting her on this organizing experience, they discovered a new way of communicating that was impactful for them both. Even the psychiatrist who referred me graciously commended the breakthrough of healing that he had seen in Nick & Anna.

It was a level even he was not able to reach during his sessions; however, I was able to reach during our at-home organizing sessions. Organizing is THAT powerful, and that is my sole purpose for writing this book.

In my mind and heart, stewarding and organizing go hand-in-hand. The foundation of this belief comes from my faith and the stewardship concept represented in the Parable of the Talents Matthew 25:14 - 28. The Lord entrusts us to steward, honor and respect what he has given us. So with that being said, I visualize a "cross" on every single item I own. From the pens in my office, to the pots in my kitchen and purses in my closet. In this spirit, the things the Lord has blessed me with will become a blessing to others once again.

This little book is like me whispering all my endless organizing secrets in your ear and your loved ones, at the same time. Your eyes will enlarge like a wise, organizing owl in excitement because all amazing things are on the verge of happening to YOU! Woohoo!

My approach to organizing will not force you to strip yourself of all your favorite belongings to conform with an extreme minimalist ethic, but you will also not be allowed to store endless years of past, poor-fitting, outdated clothing and excessive home inventory from previous decades in nifty labeled matching containers.

Instead, this is the type of organizing book where we'll work together to develop and define that "sweet spot" in the middle of both mindsets that represents you and your home values. Our work will fan the flame in you so you can watch it glow.

In the first section of the book, *Matters of the Heart,* you will define your Organizing Personality. Then in the second section, *Matters of the Mind,* new perspectives will be revealed about being mindful of what you own and its purpose in your life. In the last section, *Matters of The Hands,* you will be guided through transforming nearly every stinkin' space in your personal abode.

Finally, you will learn how to stop losing monies in your wallet and wasting time on the clock and instead kick your insecurities to the curb. The days of experiencing frustrated fails will be old news. Never again will the inner organizer fire in you fizzle out … NEVER! Instead, let's light it up people and start discovering your "Organizing Personality"…

What is YOUR Organizing Personality?

As a professional organizer, I am naturally inclined to label everything … including our organizing personalities. With that in mind, it only seemed fitting to begin by reflecting on our own personalities and behaviors around our "stuff and systems" with some light-hearted labels to which we can relate.

Before I dive into it all, let me share that each personality has its own strengths! My job and the role of this book is to help you better understand and appreciate WHY you love what you love, how it represents you, and what no longer serves a purpose in the current stage of your life.

Sounds like a game plan to go for? From this moment forward, you have officially moved into a no-guilt zone. Yes! There is no reason to waste today's current emotions and energies on decisions made in the past. That is what is soooo great about time. It literally has a *beginning* and end, every day! Ready to roll out a new day? I know I am, so let's find out which of these best personalities describes YOU! And remember, **happy days come through organized ways!**™

Fast Moving Train

Your "life train" is running you ragged because you moved from being in position as the "conductor" to now being a "passenger" on this fast-moving locomotive. You desperately want to slow down in order to figure out how your schedule got so crazy. If you don't find a solution soon, you're going to zoom past the stops and miss important life events. You are overcommitted outside the home and under committed inside the home. There is no time to complete projects that have been started—from unfinished laundry to piled-up mail. Your voicemail is full, but you can't pause long enough to clear the messages. If your position on the train doesn't adjust soon your family life will emotionally derail. You can't wait to hop off this fast-moving train and consider another vehicle that travels at a manageable pace so you can embrace your beautiful life and not let it pass you by.

Overjoyed Collector

You are a lover of all things unique, crafty, and creative. You are compelled to gather because "your things" bring you immense joy and fond memories. But your "joys" have taken over more space in your life and home than you realized. If only you had a bigger home! Your clever solution is to purchase more bookcases and organizing units to house them all. Because your floor is being used for storage rather than living space, you've created an embarrassing jungle. You eventually will need a zip line to navigate over the piles of your "joys." Whee! Once the space inside your home was filled, you moved on to the garage, then a storage unit. It's time for your joyful adventure to be re-navigated so you can begin walking on healthier, simpler trails. Life is too precious to push away close relationships because you are too embarrassed to invite guests over to visit.

Container–a–holic

You hear angels sing and heavenly harps play when you enter The Container Store. You love anything and everything that has to do with organizing. You constantly reorganize spaces using all your nifty products. Lately, you've become frustrated because after trying out your latest gadgets, you find yourself with new "organized clutter." Spaces may be organized and labeled, but they are still not efficient.

Too much work is required to use your system, and it's hard to find what you need when you need it. Even though items are put in nice, well labeled containers, it still doesn't change the fact that you don't use half of what you are storing. It's time to get raw and realistic by asking, "What is the true purpose of WHY I am electing to store this item?" It's time to stop playing "the storage game" and start streamlining your interests. Your time and money will be freed up so you can pursue and engage in an efficient and clutter-free life.

Formerly Known as Organized

Everything had its place. The house was kept tidy, bills paid on time, and laundry done promptly. Then "life happened." You transitioned into a different season of life, yet your organizing systems didn't or couldn't transition with you. You were prevented from being able to "bridge the gap" as a result of marriage, work, multiple moves, illness, or kiddos. You are now frustrated, because your best attempts to carry your skills across to the other side and get organized haven't worked.

It's time to stop trying to fit your old schedule and old systems into your new life. The sooner you embrace and acknowledge that you are in a different phase of life, the sooner you will arrive at your organized destination. It may take longer than you wanted to get there, but it is better to get things done right the first time rather than constantly wasting energy. Keep an open mind as you learn new organizing skills. Redesigning the spaces and systems you have can yield results you never thought possible. You can't get your old life back, but what you have now can be even better.

Secretive Stuffer

You desperately desire to be an organized person. It would be a dream come true to get yourself together someday, but then you ask, "Where would I start?" The idea of an organized you is appealing, but the execution is simply too overwhelming. You weren't born with natural God-given organizing skills nor taught them while growing up. Your solution is to be a "stuffer." Prior to guests visiting, you round up miscellaneous items and "stuff" them into an open drawer or cupboard. Old mail and deliveries are gathered into shopping bags and stored in the spare bedroom. The "stuffer" lives in secret. Shhh! Everyone thinks the stuffers are so organized because they hide the surface clutter, but if one was to wander off looking for something an avalanche of hidden clutter would cascade down on them.

It's time to stop living in secret and start stewarding your belongings. As you address your mess, layer by layer, endless treasure is found, from duplicate phone cords to lost parts. Ooops, there's that long-missing uncashed check and a whole stack of gift cards. You're shocked in bittersweet disbelief how much stuff you have stuffed and the generous room now available. When you reach your organized objective, you find a massive pressure has been lifted. You can't stop opening and closing doors peeking into your pretty spaces, and no need to hide your secret from guests.

Pinterest Perfectionist

Countless hours are spent with you ripping recipes from magazines or pinning projects on multiple boards. You gather organizing ideas obsessively until the point of mental exhaustion from all the DIY projects, crafty chore charts, and fancy future mudrooms you've found. You are quick to purchase the materials for your next projects, yet you never actually complete any. You want infinite things for your family, yet you rarely pause to consider if anyone needs them. Organizing skills aren't being taught to the kiddos because it's easier for you to do it yourself rather than sacrifice your perfectionist ways to teach them. Your ideas are too big, and your free time is too small. Since your standards are too high, your perfectionism fuels this obsessive cycle.

Meanwhile, you are frozen in guilt, thinking you are an inadequate provider to the family you love wholeheartedly. It's time to stop pinning yourself into the land of perfection and reassess your bucket list. Consider including your family in your projects so you can feed your inner creative side while creating family memories together. Progress, and not perfection, needs to become your new life mantra. Pass on the endless pinning and put aside the guilt so you can move forward with a fun, simple plan for completion.

Chaotic Cluttered Combo

You may be uber-organized at work but not at all at home. You could have a well-organized kitchen, yet your office is gravely infected with a paperwork virus. How is that possible? You may suffer from "multiple-organizing personality disorder." The organizing dysfunction becomes more complex when any of the above personalities combine, whether it occurs in one or more spaces. This can strike at any time and in any combination of ways and spaces.

When it does, it's time to have a serious kumbaya talk with the dominant dysfunctional personality. It's time to change those old habits that are preventing your from moving forward toward a healthier clutter-free life. Follow your gut instincts and give it up. Reflect on what you truly want for your life, your family, and your home. Recognize that every day we are grateful to be issued a brand spankin' new day. Stop obsessing on poor decisions made in the past and redirect that energy toward a new vision. Imagine the freedom! Can you feel it? Congrats! You are half way there ... now go make it real.

Needs Buttoning Up

You are pretty good at organizing your spaces, but things still do not look or feel finished to you. Just like a shirt that has lost its top buttons, you can only button it up three-fourths of the way. A few drawers and closets here and there—they look good, they work, and they function okay. Bins are mixed and matched, and supplies aren't consistently labeled so you are constantly being asked by your family where things are because they can't find them.

It bugs you big time to spend countless hours organizing to make your home "look pretty," but you are fresh out of ideas on how to achieve the finished look. If only someone could just tell you *how*, then you could confidently follow the directions to complete it yourself. If only! Your confidence and motivation will be your greatest support toward the finish line. You are so close you can practically touch it. Once you weave in the right product and systems, you will be lookin' sharp, like a well ironed shirt that is all buttoned up and ready to impress.

The Minimalist

You own one wooden spoon, one cooking pot, and two skillets. If there were a canned food drive, you would have to pull from that week's groceries because you don't overbuy. You only need and own one notepad for list making. You can shop guilt-free at Target's $1 section because you are excited to snag a super cute notepad for your upcoming friend's birthday. You then quickly wrap and mail her gift so it will arrive early. If the power went out in your home, you could still find whatever you needed because everything has a "home" and is in its place. Even though your organizing strength is to take action quickly on daily tasks, be mindful to not "rob" other family members of the organizing skill experience. All too often this type ends up *enabling* rather than *empowering* others to learn those organizing and decision-making skills that come naturally to you. Take your eager energies and channel them into teaching those who need help creating organizing systems in their life—in their way and style. People want to be like you, and you are flattered all the same. However, you ideally want them to thrive independently from you instead of being so dependent on you.

Over the years, these are the organizing personalities I've encountered most often. Do you see yourself in any or a few of these categories?

Now, we're ready to get started. **Join me in this book, and we will *Ignite the Organizer in You*. I want you to *think differently* about what you own, *why* you own it, and why it has *value* to remain in your life.**

The book is purposefully divided into three supportive Pillars that should be followed in the order presented. This will not only maximize the development of your organizational skill set but also prevent you from falling back on old habits that did not serve you.

Pillar I: Matters of the Heart teaches you how to define your Organizing Personality.

Pillar II: Matters of the Mind teaches you to think like an organizer.

In the last section, *Pillar III: Matters of The Hands,* you will apply those skills to organizing specific spaces in your home.

It is truly essential that you read through *Pillars I and II* to get your heart and mind ready so the spaces discussed in *Pillar III* can be transformed in the most efficient manner. You have the choice to tackle any space in this section in any order, but only once you have completed the foundational framework of *Pillars I and II.*

You will earn a bundle of kindling to keep your organizing flame burning within if you've successfully completed the checklist at the end of each chapter. This will help you review your newly learned skills and prove your readiness for the next step.

Ready to go? Heck, yeah!

- ✓ Visit **WurthOrganizing.com** and locate the **Shop Tab** to print your free printable set which accompany the book's teaching methods. There is also a **Resource Guide** at the back of the book that references all the suggested products and printables for each chapter.
- ✓ **If you ever feel overwhelmed, then freely flip to the last section of the book Titled** *Matters of Reference,* **where you will find The Coaching Corner: A Few Quick Wins to Conquer Anytime, to boost your confidence level right back up!**

Sign up for our *Teachable Tips Newsletter* to receive our most clever organizing methods and moments shared with clients and readers just like you!

2

BUILD YOUR
ORGANIZING TOOL KIT

Like any task, organizing requires the right tools and planning before you start. Would you walk over to set the dinner table with one clean plate but no cups or utensils? Of course not! It would be an inefficient use of time and energy to place one plate on the table and then move from cupboard to table, delivering one item at a time. It is more efficient to gather dinner necessities onto one serving tray and deliver them simultaneously. Bam!

Getting started is the hardest part for many clients. I get it. You've been making do with your situation, and other attempts at change haven't worked out. But I also know that you're reading this book, so you're motivated to make a change. You're ready to take the first step! This step will be different than what you've done before—you're going to create an Organizing Tool Kit™. As you actively build your Organizing Tool Kit and collect items for your Bin of Bins™ and Bag of Bags™ Boutique, the experience will take you from being an organizing "dreamer" into an organizing "doer."

From Dreamer to Doer

Take my client, Saundra, who dreamed of having an organized home but couldn't get started. Whenever she couldn't find something she needed, she'd buy a new version. Upon walking into her home for our initial session, you could see the cohesive design and welcoming energy of her home. There was no visible clutter.

I was not fooled for a New York minute. Saundra's home looked organized and well maintained, but I knew her secret. I asked permission to open some closet drawers and doors. She replied, "Go right ahead but be careful because things may fall down on you."

Just as expected, upon opening the nicely oiled doors, I found the many layers of life that lay beneath. "I just shove things where there is open space," Saundra explained. "I can't really find anything so sometimes it's easier to just buy another set of something, like scissors, instead of digging around to find what I need. If company is visiting, I gather everything that is left out, put it in a shopping bag, and place in the spare bedroom. I have shopping bags for who knows how many years now."

Saundra's situation is typical of the "dreamer" organizing personality who finds it easier to "stuff" their disorganization behind closed drawers and doors. Saundra travels for her job, while her husband works at home and wants a clutter-free, organized space. "I don't know where to begin, which is why I called you, because I don't want to live like this anymore."

I empathize with Saundra and others in the "stuffer" category. It's a common scenario that has been shared with Wurth Organizing hundreds of times. Despite her great storage space, Saundra can't find items she wants to use when she needs them. "It is so overwhelming," she told us. "I don't even know where I would start. Whenever I try to make progress, I just make a bigger mess and get frustrated trying to make it work. I have dish sets I don't use, mail I haven't opened, and food in the pantry I can't find when I need it. I know what I want things to look like, but I just don't know how to get there."

Organizing Tool Kit

Creating an Organizing Tool Kit will get you started on your journey from disorder to order. Don't come up with reasons why you can skip setting up the tool kit. I know that you, like Saundra, are eager to begin transforming your space. Years of experience have proven to me that without a properly packed tool kit, it will take even longer to see significant progress. Your organizing rhythm will be broken multiple times because you will be forced to stop and scavenge for needed items. Your frustration will increase and that reduces your motivation to finish. The last thing we want to see is the organizer in you ignited then fizzle out too quickly. There go your plans … up in smoke!

Instead, we will gather all the core products you will need to create a personalized Organizing Tool Kit. You don't have to find the perfect container. It is more important to focus on gathering the essentials that go in the container and then keeping it in a single, secure place. Who doesn't love the feeling of marking things off a checklist? Heck, yes! So, let's begin our checklist of essential organizing tools.

First, go on a scavenger hunt around your house gathering the CORE essentials to create your personal Organizing Tool Kit:

1. **Banker Box**

   It is the classic sturdy cardboard box historically used to store old tax files. It is easy on the back to lift, has side openings for handles, and a lid to protect your items between organizing sessions. The kitchen table is not a viable substitute, so don't even consider it! Any small-size box with a sturdy bottom, handles, and a lid will do. Between organizing sessions, cover your kit with its lid to keep out curious critters (toddlers, teenagers, spouses, and pets alike). Mine would say: "No touching; you will be gravely harmed." Protecting your tool kit means you won't have to waste time with another scavenger hunt to get started next time. Like my Italian grandmother would say … *Capisce?*

2. **Brother Label Maker**

   To me, this $35 investment is nonnegotiable for thousands of reasons. No further discussion required. Just trust me on this one! Because this is such an important tool, I want to explain more about the magic of the label maker here. The recommend the Brother P-Touch Model: PT – 1890®, which offers the best value for the money by including the label tape and batteries in its combo packaging.

I have shared this with a gazillion folks before and will share with you, too: The label maker has magical powers! No, seriously. I have seen the most stubborn clients and kiddos alike resist wanting to kick-start organization of their spaces. Then, out comes the label maker, and their mood takes a drastic change.

The label maker's instructions can be overwhelming to follow so check out my snappy sidebar on making the best labels to give you a head start and save on excessive use of label tape. First, think of each tab theme like a chapter in a book. When you want more detail about that chapter, hit the okay button to review and select more options.

How to Make the Best Labels Ever

Top 4 settings to adjust on your label maker:

1. **Font Tab** – Select "bold" so you can see labels during the day or at night when eyes get weary.
2. **Margin** – Select "narrow" to avoid wasting tape for each print-off.
3. **Label length** – Set for 3.5 instead of "max," which will adjust the font size to make it fit within your label range. The max setting causes the labels to be inconsistent and not professional looking.
4. **Underline/Frame** – All labels look best with a finished frame rather than with just a font that is floating on the surface that the label is adhered to. "Banner" is a nice classic option to select. Print different fonts for your family members in a variety of frames to place on water bottles or other belongings while you learn. This is my favorite one to master, and I love doing it with my kiddos!

3. **The Basics**
   * 1 retractable contractor-style measuring tape
   * 1 small hammer
   * 10 nails of different sizes
   * 1 clear shoe box with a lid. Clear is best so you can see all your organizing doodads inside, and you can easily grab what you need.

4. **Office Supplies**

Place the following items inside the clear shoe box:
   * 1 clipboard with your favorite writing pen/pencil attached. Trust me, you will lose it a hundred times if it is not attached with ribbon or Velcro. Been there, done that, until I attached mine.
   * 10 binder clips
   * 10 paper clips (jumbo preferred)
   * 10 rubber bands
   * 10 small adhesive mailing labels
   * 10 large adhesive mailing labels
   * 2 medium point permanent markers
   * 1 handy hole puncher
   * 1 seriously sharp scissors

5. **Kitchen Supplies**
   * 10 medium zipper style plastic bags
   * 10 large zipper style plastic bags
   * 1 roll of kitchen-sized garbage bags
   * 10 plastic handled grocery bags

* 1 roll of blue painters' tape
* 1 package of baby wipes to sanitize your items and the area as you work.

Build a Bin of Bins and Bag of Bags Boutique

Another organizing concept that I consider just as essential as the Organizing Tool Kit is a Boutique of both Bins and Bags.

This concept originated after my son, Devon, was born. I was at home and a first-time mom, yet I still wanted to implement organized systems in my family nest—the very moment an organizing idea came to me. I am not a patient person. Even my husband, Phil, jokes that the word "procrastination" doesn't exist in my vocabulary, nor in my veins. With that being said, when I wanted to create a system, I realized I had to scavenger hunt like a headless chicken under my bathroom sink, on closet shelves, or even in my recyclable trash can to find certain-sized containers.

After playing this hectic hunt-and-peck game once, this mother hen said, "Enough is enough!" Right then, I grabbed a shopping bag (that eventually graduated in size into an 18-gallon lidded tote) and labeled my newly created Wurth Organizing Container Boutique, one for bags and one for bins. Whenever I had a misfit food container with/without a lid, mini zipper pouch, or pretty leftover mason jelly jar, they were cleaned out and placed into my Boutique.

I expanded the collection with the addition of any clear, vinyl zippered bags that many pillowcases or linens come in. I would place all the smaller ones inside one large one. When the cover for my son's sleeping bag ripped—no worries for me. I just dashed to my Bag of Bags and problem solved. Do you have a toiletry travel bag filled with travel-sized liquids? Do you want an extra layer of protection for your clothes in case of spillage when traveling? I place my toiletry bag inside a vinyl pillowcase zipper bag, flip over the product description card in the front pocket, and mark the contents I need for future travels, such as daily vitamins or medications, as a reminder to pack those items for the trip. I mean really people, how efficiently savvy is that?

Daily Life Bags

This same concept also can be applied to all the daily life bags that don't currently have a purpose in your life such as: draw string bags, duffel bags, beach bags, and backpacks. Again, pick the largest size and house all the others inside. To save space and reduce cord tangling, roll up the soft ones, wrap tightly with a few rubber bands, and then place inside the master bag, which houses your main inventory.

The more I used my convenient onsite Boutique, the more I realized this idea was not only stinkin' brilliant (thank you very much for agreeing with me!), but I immediately resolved three organizing problems:

✱ **Gained Storage Space** – Why keep an empty beauty zipper pouch stored in a space where it doesn't currently serve a purpose? By storing all the bins and bags together, I gained square footage that allows for more important, nonnegotiable items to be stored there instead, such as a back stock of toilet paper or bathroom products under the sink.

* **Neutralize the Products Theme** – When that product (e.g., bathroom zipper pouch) is kept in a certain space, you automatically think that product should *belong and be used* in that exact space. You are in fact *limiting that product's full potential* when it could be better utilized in another space. For instance, if I was organizing my office and needed a something to house on-the-go tech cords, then I would walk directly to my Boutique, find a zipper pouch (which was once stored in the bathroom), and then finish organizing my office space.

* **Try Before You Buy** – No scavenger hunt is required when you have a Bin and Bags Boutique, and money is seamlessly saved in the process. By placing the on-the-go tech cords in a zipper pouch, I can try the concept out and see if the size and shape work for my initial needs. If the product style and shape work, then I scored big right away. If I love the pouch concept, yet need a larger version, then I can confidently purchase one that is appropriately sized and restock the existing one back into my Boutique.

Future Organizer Alert!!!

Before I start any client session, I give my clients the task of creating their own Bag and Bin Boutique. Often, the volume easily would fill half a guest room floor or car bay. I am 100 percent fine with a large inventory being stored in one place until all their organizing projects are completed to their satisfaction. Only then are they advised to keep at most 1-2 totes worth of bins or bags and donate the excess inventory. My hope is that the sheer volume of your Boutique (which may look like an indoor mall) is not added to under any set of circumstances unless absolutely, desperately necessary!

Thank you for taking the first step and putting your faith in me to guide you this far. I am beyond proud of you for investing in yourself by organizing your own Organizing Tool Kit and Bin and Bags Boutique. These essential elements will allow you to approach spaces with professional tools.

You've got the organizing groove on now!

You have earned your bundle of kindling to keep your organizing flame burning within if you've successfully completed the following:

❑ Bought a Brother label maker and stocked it with batteries.
❑ Know the basics of working the label maker—set the font, label length, and printing a variety of decorative frames.
❑ Stocked the remaining items in your Organizing Tool Kit and checked the list—TWICE!
❑ Marked "Do not touch or you will be harmed" on your tool kit box so others don't snag your core tools for their project while you try to complete yours.

❑ You feel satisfied knowing how much you have completed already by building your tool kit.
❑ You have established a nice (but not excessive) inventory of Bins and Bags in your Boutique.

By completing this chapter, you've created a lifeline towards your organized life. I envision you climbing the steps on the high diving board. You have walked in faith, trusting me as you step toward the very end of the board. You have been properly equipped, and you are ready to leap off and soar headfirst into your organizing projects. What if you do a belly flop? Who cares! You jumped off the dang diving board!

What if your dive isn't perfect like the other divers? Still don't care! You know it is more about progress than perfection. What if I drown in my clutter? You won't because I am your on-duty lifeguard to lead you safely back to the right steps. Following my strategic steps will guide you until you feel confident enough to dive into your organizing projects on your own.

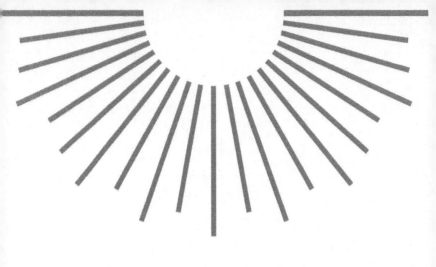

MATTERS
—OF THE—
MIND

BECOME A MASTER GATEKEEPER

Stop Giving Keys to Your Home for Others to Access

Your home is your sanctuary from the bustling outside world. It is literally the only place where you can retreat. You can pay for peace and quiet at a hotel or spa, but eventually your family will come looking for you. Your home is designed to be a place where you can refresh your spirit, renew your energy, and reflect on your day. When your space is organized, it brings calmness out of the chaos of everyday life.

To enter your haven, you mostly use a traditional key to open the door. As the gatekeeper to your home, you have shared a few extra keys with loved ones, or what I will call key masters—those you trust in your home. Now imagine if one of your key masters shares about a thousand copies of your keys with multiple people from multiple stores! All these new key masters can charge into your home and bring with them their clothes, mail, receipts, work papers, toys, books, and other random doodads.

You may ask, "What the heck is going on here? I didn't give you a key to my home! I didn't grant you permission to enter it! You can't just barge in here and leave your stuff all over. I want you to leave now! And please take all your stuff with you!" Slam goes the door.

Master Gatekeeper Training

Gatekeeping was a challenging concept for our client, Tina (An Overjoyed Collector), who is an avid collector of teapots. Over the years, Teapot Tina's spare bedroom swarmed into a cyclone of clutter. She asked me to transform the space that had become a catchall for storage into a combo guest bedroom and hobby room. Tina wanted to use the space to create pincushions inside her antique teapots. I loved the idea and wanted to help her kick this project into action. I asked her how much project time she wanted to devote per month to the pincushions. Tina wanted to start out with one teapot pin cushion per month.

We gathered all her teapots together and then stood back in silence while waiting for Tina's response. As she pondered the three overflowing boxes of teapots, Tina exclaimed, "Whoa! I didn't realize I had gathered so many teapots."

There were three boxes because Tina had yet to unlock her gatekeeping skills. Together, we chose the teapots she most wanted to work on, decreasing her inventory to about three-quarters of one box. The rest were sent to consignment. Teapot Tina went from overwhelmed to excited about her pincushion project.

If she had learned about gatekeeping sooner, Teapot Tina would have spent less time collecting and dedicated more time to enjoying her pincushion craft. That's because once clutter enters your home, you have to decide whether to read it, file it, shred it, share it, polish it, maintain it, clean it, discard it, donate it, or sell it. You've signed yourself up for another full-time job, making decisions about all the items flowing into your home. Most of us would say, "No way, I am not interested in this new job. What can I do about it?"

The initial step to becoming a Master Gatekeeper is awareness. You need to recognize that for every item that enters your home, a decision about it must be made. Second, it is best to make that decision *the moment* you are acquiring an item rather than *after* it has entered your home. This means turning off the "when" setting and turning on the "now" setting.

OK, take a deep breath. When you or loved ones bring something into your home, then you have, indeed, granted access for any items you or they leave behind—from restaurant menus you take home but never read, to recipes you tear out or pin yet never make.

If you don't regularly use something in your daily life, then it is clutter. Period. No exception. No further reasoning or negotiating required.

When decisions become repeatedly delayed, belongings will continue to build, layer upon layer. Ultimately, this accumulation makes it even more difficult to catch up. You are a smart person. Whether you are emotionally challenged or physically challenged, whether you are 5, 15, or 55 years old, I believe, in my heart, that you—and every single person on this planet—are capable of making solution-oriented decisions and placing things where they belong.

One-Minute Rule™

If kindergartners can place their belongings in a classroom cubby, then surely you can put away your things, too. The best way to do this is by making small changes in your daily routine that then become habits. This is easiest if you follow the one-minute rule. If a task can be done in one minute or under, then it's something you should do immediately. A good way to start this habit is to make it part of your routine. For instance, before you head out the door in the morning, you can make sure that you always put the hairbrush back in the drawer or replace the empty toilet paper roll with a fresh one or make your bed! Accomplishing these quick tasks creates a habit and gives you the knowledge and confidence that you can be a Master Gatekeeper.

As Master Gatekeeper, when you see something that needs to be done, ask yourself, "Is a task required?" Then, answer yes or no. If the answer is yes, you are the decision-maker, and if the task can be accomplished now, then do it! No excuses, no delays. If the task is not done, it will lead to 1,000 laters. I will get to that later, and that later, and etc. However, if a task requires more than one minute, then transform the task into a project and place it in the designated area of your office with other more complex projects.

One-Minute Rule Scenario

Here's a scenario that demonstrates the effectiveness of the One-Minute Rule in mastering gatekeeping for your home:

You head to the local drug store to pick up your monthly prescription. The pharmacist asks for your email address and you quickly provide it not asking how it will be shared. The pharmacist hands over your prescription in a paper sack, which is placed inside a plastic bag. You also get a receipt and three coupons that the cash register automatically pumps out to loyal customers. Typical customers take the meds sack, a flyer about a health expo to give to a friend, and then shove the receipt and its coupons into the plastic shopping bag to be dealt with later when they get home. (Remember what I said about turning off "when" and turning on "now?")

Now, watch how a Master Gatekeeper does it.

A Master Gatekeeper would kindly ask the pharmacist the purpose of sharing your email address. If the gatekeeper elects to not receive coupon offers via email, then states how their email is personal information and prefer not to share it, but thank you for asking.

The pharmacist hands over your prescription and is told to skip placing it in a plastic bag to protect the environment. The gatekeeper would then step aside at the counter to let all the huffing, impatient people in line have their turn while taking 10 seconds to sort the various items. The trained gatekeeper circles the credit card type, date, and total for future bookkeeping then takes a quick picture of the flyer and texts it to her friend.

Our gatekeeper then glances through the coupons and expiration dates to see if she would really, really, really buy those items before the coupons expire. If not, then the smart gatekeeper hands the coupons back to the pharmacist saying, "I want to pass these along to another customer." This may result in a confused look from the pharmacy staff, but good gatekeepers get over the odd glares quickly.

Lastly, trained gatekeepers open the prescription sack, recycle the endless instructions along with the sack, because they take the medication regularly and don't need to read the pamphlet. Finally, our Master Gatekeeper places the medication into a purse/satchel and leaves the store with a stellar smile, knowing that when she gets home, the only task is to put away the medicine.

Dang, that's good! By doing 10 seconds of Master Gatekeeping at the store, you will get into the healthy habit of making quicker decisions while avoiding being sucked into the "I will deal with it later cycle." Later usually joins forces with other "later friends" left in your car, your home, and elsewhere in your life. Later often morphs into "much later" before eventually transforming into "never." The sooner you grasp the "Now is better than later" concept, the sooner you gain control of your home, and you can banish all those key masters with their excessive items.

Look Who is Master of Their House Now! Yes!

You have become a Master Gatekeeper and earned your bundle of kindling to keep your organizing flame burning if you successfully completed the following:

- ❏ Shopped in at least 10 stores and left with only the absolutely necessary and truly needed items.
- ❏ You can explain and have demonstrated the One-Minute Rule at least 20 times throughout your daily endeavors.
- ❏ You have politely said "no" to cashiers, sales people, or other service folks when offered coupons, flyers, or marketing materials that you know you won't use.
- ❏ You protect your email address like it was your social security number, telling any sales rep, "No, I'm sorry. My email is private information, and I prefer not to share it."
- ❏ You have consistently been discarding trash as quickly as possible from your purse/satchel and more mindful of what needs to be placed inside of it.

Congratulations! You're a Master Gatekeeper, protecting yourself and your home from unnecessary clutter. You're now ready to move on to becoming a Master Decision-Maker.

4

BECOME A MASTER DECISION-MAKER

Do-it-Now Decisions vs. 1,000 Laters

Do you recognize how quick and effective decision-making can be? You've already started! By following the one-minute rule and doing things now rather than in 1,000 laters (when it will be a much bigger undertaking), you have shown that you are a gatekeeper capable of making decisions. We are now going to apply that capability more broadly across multiple aspects of daily life.

I believe in my heart—10,000 percent—that you can and will become a Master Decision-Maker. This is not a complicated concept. Like when you became a Master Gatekeeper, it simply takes daily practice and consistent repetition until it becomes natural.

Why lug trash from your car inside to drop on the counter when, instead, you can drop it in the trash can in the garage?

A light bulb just flickered in your brain, right? Why toss keys on the table when you can hang them on the key rack? Buzz ... light bulb again! Instead of kicking shoes off at the door, head straight to the bedroom, and store them in the closet. Buzz, buzz. Light bulb! Look how brilliant you have become. I am so very proud of you and how much you have accomplished in such a short period of time!

During most organizing sessions, clients confess to me the following recurring statement: "I am just so disorganized! I can't seem to get it together. I have piles of things everywhere." I could record this phrase, and future clients could save energy by hitting the replay button rather than repeating the same frustrations. I empathize with them because their situation is common, and they are not alone in feeling overwhelmed. Once they understand my psychology-based approach toward creating organized systems for their home, hope blossoms.

Making a Change

One of our clients, Cadence, came to us after years of frustration. Her organizing personality was a "Chaotic Cluttered Combo" of a Fast-Moving Train and a Container-a-Holic. Her life was so busy that she couldn't slow down to get organized. But she kept buying organizing items, which would collect dust in her garage, while she hoped to eventually make use of them. Cadence was exhausted, overwhelmed, and didn't know where to start. She said, "I don't know where things are, and I don't know my schedule for today nor tomorrow."

At Wurth Organizing, we compare clutter in the home to a delicate layer cake. The clutter represents many layers of life's activities and experiences. Some layers were created over months, while others span a few years and some perhaps even decades. Everyone's layer cake is unique to their life's minutiae. Having layers of life surround you does not mean you're disorganized; it simply means it is time to become a Master Decision-Maker. That's it. You can stop beating yourself up in the boxing ring over what you have been calling disorganization and put your energy into knocking out clutter with some heavy-hitting decision-making.

Cadence called when she was ready to stop beating herself up and was ready to start making progress. We explained that her motivation to change and openness to learning new organizing skills is all that is required for success. By merely connecting with me, the rest is just stuff that needs to be dealt with through our ongoing sessions.

It can be emotionally difficult for any individual to embrace their current situation, put aside their pride, stare straight into their cluttered piles of shame, and then bravely dial our number. But, right after making that call, hope begins. After our first session, Cadence told us, "I feel so much better already, just getting it off my chest and just talking about all this." So, now you can take the next step on the journey, just like Cadence did.

One-Minute Rule in Practice

We have talked about specific organizing personalities, guarding your home as Master Gatekeeper, and the power of making decisions now versus later. Hot diggity dog! Time to pump your fist in the air and watch the volume of things coming into your home gradually dwindle.

Now, we're going to combine all these skills and practice decision-making in real life. We'll start by applying it to your layer cake and your daily activities. Let's put on our clutter-busting gloves and knock this thing out for good.

Let's repeat our rule: "If you can do a task in one minute or less, then do it right then. Bam! Done! It's outta' here!" Move on to the next task and the next and the next and the next. You will be amazed how much can be accomplished, one minute at a time, by doing it in the now rather than later.

Let's start with tips on how to sort through a pile of mail in one minute or less.

❑ **Review unwanted mailers and magazines** – Tear off the back page that has the company's toll-free number and the yellow and blue source codes used for customer mailing. Take 30 seconds to call and request your name be removed from their distribution list. Ask if they have sister companies and request removal from those mailing lists as well. One call can do it all.

❑ **Recycle junk postcards** – Some mailers you can't control receiving because they get distributed based on zip codes.

❑ **Unpaid bills** – Open the statement, quickly review included inserts and toss if the inserts serve no purpose. Circle the date, account number, staple the statement together, paperclip it to the return envelope, and recycle the mailing envelope. Because a task is required and will take more than one minute, place the bill in your future Action Required box. We will deal with converting to online bill pay when we discuss organizing your home office.

- **Paid bills or credit card statements** – Use the same process as above, but the statement needs reconciling for bookkeeping or taxes. Gather related receipts and binder clip them to the correct statement. Because you have already mastered gatekeeping for your past purchases by circling the card type, date, and total, your reconciling process will be extraordinarily efficient when you are ready.

- **Coupons** – I only cut and keep the coupon for my kids' haircuts because that is truly the only one I will use. It is placed into my wallet clipped with their budget money for the month. Only save the coupons you know you actually will use, attach them to the grocery list or put them in your wallet to use.

- **Vendor info for future projects** – Put aside in a designated area to discuss with your loved ones at another point in time. Phil and I have found a Thursday night or Sunday night is a good time for us to review logistics for the upcoming weekend or school events.

- **Things to read** – Designate an area for your reading materials. I have to honestly acknowledge having only one to two hours a week to devote to leisurely reading. I use my Master Gatekeeping skills accordingly so that I don't pile things up. Otherwise, I am delaying decision-making. The pile lurks in the corner guilting me that I am not reading it. Ditch the guilt and embrace the reality by spending your time doing what you love. Consider canceling your subscriptions or transferring them to a loved one's household. Want to continue to receive them until the subscription expires? Gather your lurking piles, black out your personal address info with a Sharpie, and dash out to the drive-through of your local library and drop them off so they can be readily enjoyed by others in your community.

❑ **Items that need to be reviewed by you** – Only put aside items you *really, really, really* think you will attend. Take a quick glance at your calendar and the events that surround that date period. Will you be on overload if you attend? It is better to RSVP with "maybe" and explain that you are awaiting confirmation on other scheduled events that may conflict. Promise to be respectful and keep them posted, however. A maybe response is better than no response to the host.

❑ **Items that need to be reviewed with loved ones** – Keep one place and one pile where you manage items for this purpose. Do not have one pile in every room or on every surface for each family member in your home. If you adhere to just having one single pile for each person, then it will get done!

I prefer a clipboard versus a pile of purpose. The paper virus can't spread when clipped down and it makes for easy surface cleaning.

✳ **For my hubby:** I place his clipboard on top of our kitchen breakfast bar. When he comes home after dinner (not right as he enters the door), we can quickly review those items. If those items require more than the standard one-minute discussion, then we "table" that discussion for our next scheduled Family Review.

* **For my kiddos:** Their clipboards are placed on the homework table in the kitchen. That way, when I sit with them after school, we address the items on their board in addition to the homework tasks due for the week.

* **The Maybe Pile:** If you are stumped on how to handle an item, then place it in a maybe pile. When you're done sorting your mail batch, review that pile again. I guarantee a clearer decision can be made in that next round.

Organizing is a constant process of reaction and adjustment to activities experienced in daily life. Every decision avoided has consequences that eventually cause confusion—day after day, layer upon layer. Awareness of your decisions is the flaming core of your organizing process and that flame must burn strongly and not fizzle.

In the beginning of your organizing ignition process, you will experience a few rounds of volume reduction. You will make bulk quality decisions and, as a result, reduce the overall volume around you. This bulk effort sets you up to make your decisions more quickly and prepares you to make even more challenging decisions. Round and round and round you will go until you reach your final decision-making round for a particular space … and, boy, does it feel great to be there!

Way to Nail Down Making So Many Decisions!

You have become a Master Decision-Maker and earned another bundle of kindling to keep your organizing flame burning within if you successfully completed the following:

❏ Catch yourself in the moment of making a good decision or recognize when you are not making one. It is the awareness of the activity or lack thereof that matters most.

❏ Power through a typical batch of mail—dividing decisions into ones you tackle immediately and ones you legitimately need to complete later.

❏ Review and reconcile your bank and/or credit card statements with your ready-to-go, tax-categorized, circled receipts. Once all charges are accounted for, then statements and corresponding receipts are scanned together for future record keeping and are ready for the paper shredded shortly after.

❏ Pass on opening any coupon mailer packs or magazines knowing there are no services you need discounts on that month.

❏ Pass on keeping any vendor promotional information unless you have serious interest to take action on a current project in the next 90 days. Otherwise, decide to enter the company website and phone number into your phone as a future contact.

❏ Pass on excessively adding to your "Things to Read" pile. Finally, you have become raw and honest with yourself by accurately calculating the amount of time you can devote to reading articles and/or books for leisure. You know excessive gathering and storage of reading material serves no purpose, and you feel at peace taking a pass on participating.

By completing this chapter, you've gained significant confidence in your ability to make more quality decisions, and more often. This shift in mindset is beyond awesome ... it is epic! Imagine the pre-frontal cortex of your brain bench pressing its muscles right now—one decision, two decisions, three decisions—serious form and flex action you got going on!

What if you only made one decision? Congrats because one is still more than zero, right? And two decisions will be next and then three and so forth.

What if my brain just can't make a decision because it is frozen with frustrated fails? I get you, but I am also here to get you moving forward. Following my lead to the next chapter will guide you until you feel self-assured enough to press on into more organizing projects on your own.

5

INCREMENTALISM, NOT PERFECTIONISM

The Fastest Way to Get Unstuck is to Strive Forward

There are usually fantastical organizing visions that frolic in our heads. Around and around and around loop these visions of perfection. You tear out magazine images and pin projects onto endless Pinterest boards in hopes of transforming certain spaces in your home. But, at some point, you realize your future dream space has not moved out of dream mode and into reality. Be wary of slowly backing yourself into the "I will be happy when _____ mentality."

This approach is unlikely to get you on a path towards true happiness. Instead, it is more likely to create a never-ending cyclical state of busyness versus progression. You plan, organize a little, and then it doesn't work as you had hoped. Eventually, you are emotionally and mentally stripped down, worn out from organizing exhaustion. You are also fresh out of finding products and the right book to teach you the latest organizing method. It's not like you aren't trying, but nothing is working and that can easily lead to madness. But why?

Life is and will forever be changing and unpredictable. If you place your hopeful dreams on situations you cannot control, then you likely will delay jumpstarting any project. Not quite the fairytale ending you were hoping for, right? We must choose joy and embrace our current living situation. Choose to have a happy, grateful heart with every breath of daily life we are given. From this place of peace, you can begin a step-by-step journey to apply that to the space around you.

To begin, you need to shift your focus from finding the right image online, the right organizing system, or the perfect custom piece for a family member. These actions distract you from making progress by focusing on a perfect finished project. They delay your progress and enjoyment of a space because it doesn't take into account the smaller steps that are needed to attain the finished project. It can be disheartening to have an unfulfilled perfectionist vision.

Progress Not Perfection

Let's say you want to create a fantastic homework and hobby room for yourself and your kiddos. After more clippings and more pins placed on boards, you find yourself exhausted from hours of obsessing about making the space perfect. You have aggressively and sadistically robbed yourself from engaging in projects you love and quality time with your loved ones.

Meanwhile, your family projects continue to spread like messy mayonnaise on a variety of kitchen and dining room surfaces. Sadly, your future homework and hobby room has been relegated to a warehouse of dreams and supplies for "that one perfect day" when the organizing stars align in picture-perfect format.

Your bar is set so stinking high you would have to be an Olympic pole vaulter to soar over it. You are probably not in this organizing dilemma to "go for the gold." It's time to step down from your perfectionist podium and stand firmly on the ground where you can evaluate your raw self and situation. When we focus primarily on perfection during the early stages of a multilayered project, then we are effectively prohibiting ourselves from making significant progress.

The Dark Side

How do I know this is true? Personal experience, my friends, personal experience. Through some counseling and anxiety reduction awareness sessions, I finally was able to destroy my need for perfection. It was right after my eldest son was born that I started working with a counselor who had experienced working with children and adults with anxiety and ADHD.

He walked me through a comparison concept called "incremental validity." At the time, I would not invest in any activity and give a measly 100 percent effort, because in my mind, it wasn't good enough, though neither was 110 percent effort. I was only happy when my bar was set at 111 percent and when I was exceeding my own falsely made expectation levels. This sounded reasonable and very doable in my perfectly folded origami mindset. Hilarious, right? If I methodically planned and organized my tasks enough, then I could easily reach the 111 percent mark and then it would be correctly classified as successful in my mind. Oh, me!

I had a bittersweet experience (aka, anxiety meltdown) after planning and hosting my niece's first birthday party at our home. My sister has a low-key, easygoing, just-wing-it type of personality, so this pressure was all brought on by *moi*. The party was in June, which is Death Valley blazing hot at 115 degrees in Arizona. Not only did I clean the house, prep food, handle decor and desserts, I also decided the food and decor needed to be extended to the outside pool area. No sane person would voluntarily sit outside in that heat unless they desire some funky sunburns as they eat birthday cake.

My counselor respectfully asked me, "Danielle, if you only did 90 percent of your task list, would the party be equally as successful?"

"Well, yes," I had to reluctantly admit. *"The only person who would know that I hadn't completed what was on my list would be me."*

"What if you only did 80 percent of your task list? Would the party still be equally as successful?" *"Oh, yes! Only I would know what wasn't completed."*

"Did people not enjoy themselves because you didn't do those extra tasks that pushed you into emotional and physical exhaustion?" *"No, not at all. It was a great party, and people enjoyed themselves. I was just too busy dashing around and didn't really hang out with everyone because of it."*

"Most people likely do 60 percent to 70 percent of what you offered at the party, so you already have gone above and beyond the average person's output in kindly hosting your niece's party." *"But Dr., I am not an average person, and I will not lower my standards because people choose to give mediocre efforts."*

"Let me ask you, would you have enjoyed yourself more as the hostess who calmly mingled with your guests versus being so frantic to serve everyone? Are people coming to the party to celebrate the birthday or to judge you and your hostess abilities?" *"No, not at all. They are coming to be with me, so we can celebrate my niece's birthday as a family."*

I walked out of my counselor's office that day relieved and forever changed. I experienced an epiphany in my soul that I so desperately needed. I learned to be aware of my actions for future projects and began to recognize the beginnings of what my hubby and I jokingly started calling "going to the dark side." When planning my kiddos' birthday parties, I enjoy making the cupcake toppers and all the coordinating decor doodads to make their parties quite the festive bash. I embraced what I was doing, and the memories being made with them and for them. We took pictures along the way because for me that was equally part of the experience and not the picture-perfect finish line. If it didn't get Plan A done, then I learned to be fine accepting Plan B. Often, I realized I likely needed to settle and accept Plan C, for that is how scenarios unfolded.

Everything for me mentally shifted forever when I asked myself...

"If God is divine and perfect and I am human and flawed, then why am I seeking to achieve something unobtainable, nor sustainable ?

My anxiety can still sometimes go to the "dark side," which causes me to lash out toward my family helpers. It takes ongoing practice to master "incremental validity" and know when "good enough" is truly "good enough" and when "above and beyond" is required. I also surprisingly noticed, after this epiphany, that "done" felt 100 times better than a project being drawn out for decades to complete, just so I could check another box off my endless to-do list. By focusing on what I can control with my present energy and funds versus what I cannot control was so relieving and revealing at the same time.

Steps for Successful Progress

The Pinterest Perfect pressure is lifted, though I need to be forever vigilant to prevent myself from sliding over to "the dark side." Here are the steps for you to take to avoid that same cycle of perfection versus progress:

Step 1 – Put down the pole vault. Stop what you are doing, step away from your current cyclical perfectionist state of madness and lower the bar. Instead of aiming for Olympic-level pole vault bar heights, think of smaller heights that will move you forward. First step? Think about a space you want to undertake and write down the top five reasons WHY you desire to create organizing systems within it.

If it will be a shared space, ask your loved ones and add their top five reasons as well. I guarantee you will be surprised to hear some of their answers, which will help motivate you more. I know it may seem silly, but please write them in this book now. If you feel you would "ruin" the book by writing in it, then write it on a sticky note and put it on the page instead.

My #1 WHY: _____

My #2 WHY: _____

My #3 WHY: _____

My #4 WHY: _____

My #5 WHY: _____

Step 2 – Be coachable. Learning new skills and approaches will be required for you to make significant progress. Be patient as you learn new ways and habits. As you gain confidence, you will eventually be able to easily throw a leg over the pole and put some happy feet in your steps. On your next round, you will be able to hop over the bar, gaining even more confidence and seeing even more progress.

Step 3 – Look around with a new perspective. See what you can do to make progress at this exact point in time. Do you have a six-foot table or spare interior door to place on top of a table that can be set up in your craft room? Before I invested in a craft table for my office, I used a six-foot table to see if I liked the light and positioning. That table was my families' workhorse for over a year. I busted out well over a hundred handmade birthday cards for my clients while my kiddos finished school projects alongside me. I didn't have the funds to buy chairs and didn't know if this table concept was a go, so I carried home two wrought iron stools from my neighbor's bulk trash one day with pride for I knew exactly where they would be placed.

Step 4 – Devise creative organizing systems. Quickly! Don't have the funds for that Pottery-Barn-Perfect Lazy Susan-style carousel to house your crafting supplies? Grab a shoebox and place inside six tall Solo cups that can house twistable crayons, pencils, markers, brushes, scissors, and erasers. It is better to test a system by setting it up in a functional way, then focus on the fancy with a later upgrade! Make changes one step at a time.

As you work with the system, you will also be able to untangle any kinks, such as "I don't use this product as much as I thought, but I use this other one instead." A final storage solution may need to be shaped differently or require more open space in a drawer, etc.

There is a tremendous benefit in following this process. You start and create a solution, then by using the space, you can make tweaks and adjustments to improve your system. Your idea evolves so that you use the space more effectively and you can reflect on what you've learned in the process. In the second half of this book, we will go into greater detail about how to transform a variety of spaces.

Serious strides taken, one increment at a time!

You have overcome perfectionism and earned another bundle of kindling to keep your organizing flame burning within if you have successfully completed the following:

❏ You have read this chapter and have had your perfection epiphany. Now, there is no turning back to your old mindset. Your perfectionist pole vault is placed on the ground, the high jump bar is significantly lowered, and you have hopped over it to the other side with an Olympic smile beaming on your face. Queen's song "We Are the Champions" is playing in your head.

❏ You understand "Try before you buy." You have refrained from purchasing more organizing doodads that only add to your existing volume and organizing inventory. What if it was free? Then try it out immediately to see if it will be functional. If not, then drag it to the end of your driveway and put a lovely sign marked free with a smiley. The item will be used by another in your community more readily than it can be stored for years without purpose in your home.

❏ Return all new items that serve no purpose in your current life. Can't find the receipt? No problem. Confidently tell the cashier you cannot locate the receipt and are completely fine with a store credit. If you positively must purchase something at that store that you desperately need at that very moment or the sky will fall, then do so. Fine! But I am telling you that you better stinking use the item or you are just faking yourself out by justifying the reason for this new purchase. Be sure and file the receipt under the vendor's name for safe keeping—just in case it turns out you didn't need it after all. (I promise not to say, "I told you so.")

❑ Return items to the people they belong to. Do you have books that need returning to the library? Supplies to be brought into your workplace? Clothes that need dropping off at a friend's or a gift that needs to be wrapped and shipped? Get everyone else's inventory out of your space. Utilize your decision-making skills on another level, and you will feel so empowered and fabulous that you may consider howling at the moon!

❑ Identify items that are obviously donatable. You no longer sew or have a vegetable garden and don't plan to in the future. You have the following three options:

1) Think about whether you know anyone who would readily use your sewing machine or tools. Then, text or call them offering it and try to hand it off within the week.

2) Contact a vendor you use (such as your alteration lady or gardener) and see if they would barter for the machine/tools, maybe in lieu of charging you for those pants that needed hemming or tree that needs trimming. Call them right away, ask if they have an interest in the deal, and move forward.

3) If you are not interested in options 1 or 2, then move straight to donation. Make the trip even more worthwhile by gathering other donatable items. Wrap bags tightly in a knot so you

don't second guess your excellent decision-making skills. Mark each bag or box with the organization's name for pick up or drop off.

Congratulations! In this chapter, you've learned to shift your mindset. Instead of focusing on a perfect, final solution, you are looking at the steps along the way. These are much easier to accomplish and help you stay focused on getting to the finish line by giving you smaller goals along the way. At this point, your organizer flame is burning bright! Remember, done will always feel better than delayed perfection. Try it, and you will see and feel the difference.

6

KICKING ACE: MASTERING THE FOUR A'S OF ORGANIZING

In the past 12 years as a professional organizer, I have yet to change my Four A's of Organizing™ for tackling a space. The methodology has demonstrated its success with hundreds of organizing clients over the years. Once you master the order and understand the reasoning, your level of organizing skills will be altered forever. Here are the secrets:

* **Assess** the space and its function.

* **Attack** by separating items into four piles–keep, consign, donate, and maybe.

* **Assign** an organized system; learn and use my P.O.P. Method™ when selecting completion products.

* **Accountable** to yourself, your family, and your home to complete and maintain one space at a time.

By now, you realize that I enjoy learning and teaching others using analogies. For this chapter, it seems fitting to use baseball as I describe the order of importance as well as the reasoning behind the Four A's. Even though baseball moves too slowly for this hard-core soccer mama, the analogy hits a home run.

Hit, Run, Strike Out

Like players waiting in a dugout, you are ready to step up your organizing game. You can smell the hotdogs in the grandstand and visualize cotton candy dreams of a more organized life when your projects move from dream phase to done phase. It's your turn at bat. You spring from the dugout because you are dying to hit this ball (also known as the organizing challenge) out of the ballpark. You aggressively hit the first pitch, and it soars over the fence. You fist pump, shouting, "YES!" In your enthusiasm, you bolt straight to third base, turn, and then run home. You gleefully do a funky chicken happy dance only to hear the umpire spit out: "Your home run didn't count! You skipped first and second base. You're OUT!"

You slam down your baseball cap in anger. What? You hit a killer ball, and it doesn't count? Frustrated, you reluctantly pick up your cap and head dejectedly to the dugout. You tell yourself it must be the bat, because if you had the right bat, then the home run would have counted. No worries, because you already have selected a newer, better quality bat.

Again, it is your turn to bat, and you smack another ball out of the park. Again, you charge towards third base and back to home. In the middle of your happy chicken dance, the umpire walks over wildly waving his sweaty hands and shouts, "No score. You're out!"

Are you kidding me? This time you justify missing first and second base by telling yourself the umpire needs his head examined. This hit, run, strike out scenario continues, play after play, until you throw down your hat in defeat. Maybe the issue wasn't the bat, but your cleats? Yes, that's it! You just need to find a better pair of cleats to make you run faster, then you will score that well-deserved home run. *Unfortunately, you are missing successful hits not because of your sports equipment, but because you need a more successful strategy.*

Now, translate this analogy to your approach in finding a nifty organizing drawer or basket solution for your master closet. You spring into your car and drive straight to your personal organizing heaven—The Container Store®. You enthusiastically fill your shopping cart with a wonderful array of colorful organizing bins, baskets, and totes, and then head home. You do cathartic cartwheels in celebration as you carry your gorgeous supplies to the closet. Then, your enthusiasm dies.

The doors on your closet won't shut because you purchased the wrong size containers. You didn't **assess your space and function** by measuring your closet and taking photos before your shopping spree on Aisle 3. This means you also failed to **assign your system**. Your solutions are either too tall or too small to store the volume of clothing and keepsakes you have protected since elementary school. Arggggghh! What the heck? You went to the right store, you bought plenty of nifty organizing solutions so your closet could look catalog perfect, but you wasted your energy because your pretty gadgets did not solve the problem.

You are back in the hit, run, and strike out scenario again, until you throw down your clipboard in frustration for the last time, telling yourself that you are a terrible organizer, a terrible person/mother/father/grandparent, and your only choice is to spend your remaining days on earth living in an anxious, shame-filled, cluttered home. You feel you let down your team and family—again. You grab a box of Cracker Jack®, looking for a consolation prize in the bottom of the box.

This is a common battle between clutter and confusion. These endless instances of what I call layers of life build up around you and every space in your home. You elect to give up, leaning your bat against the wall and shoving your clipboard to the back of the cabinet drawer.

Over the years, I have seen a consistent pattern. This story tugs on my heart and tears me apart. There is consistent sadness when clients don't find the right solutions. It's a madness that consumes many of our clients, no matter their demographic, financial background, or season of life. During an initial consult visit, clients often describe to me the spaces in their home, their shameful scars they tried to heal, and then ask me "Danielle, do you think you can help me?"

This is my favorite part because I know I have the knowledge, expertise, and systems to successfully ignite the organizer in them and to teach them how to score big while avoiding running in the wrong direction. Once you learn why your play didn't succeed, we can move on to learning how to make it work for you. No matter the volume, no matter how many failed attempts, you deserve and can have a healthy, clutter-free life.

New Playbook for Organizing

ASSESS PHASE

Assess your space and its function. This is when you ask questions and take notes. This is most definitely not the "drive straight to the store" or "hop online in search of the right product to solve my problem right now" phase. Imagine yourself arriving on a crime scene of horrific proportions of disorganization. You are the clever detective merely taking notes, taking pictures, and gathering clues. You are not typing a final report on the scene and stating who did it, right? No! It's the same thing as an organizer; you don't need to have all the answers yet. Invest at least 15–20 minutes and spend it assessing your space and its function. Now, it's time to play detective in your own home, aka crime scene of disorganization!

Practice Organizing Project – WWSBD. WWJD is a popular acronym that stands for "What would Jesus do?" When you are ready to act on something, this is a common phrase you might use to pause and reflect … WWJD? It forces you to rethink your actions and behaviors. I say we take a spin on that popular catchphrase and give it an organizing twist … What Would a Starbucks® Barista Do? (WWSBD) All too often, my guru girls and I notice that our clients make at least four stops in the kitchen just to make a single cup of java. A Starbucks barista would never work that inefficiently.

In this scenario, you are going to ignite your inner organizer and tackle a small project to practice the Four A's and create your own barista beverage station!

Let's apply the Four A's and streamline your coffee or tea-making by creating your own barista station.

Assess the space and its function. Your coffee maker sits on the kitchen counter. The filters are stored in the cupboard in a paper box. The floppy coffee bag sits on a shelf in the pantry, while the tea boxes are kept on another. The sugar bag can be found with the baking supplies under your island placed inside a Ziploc bag because it makes a mess every time you open/close the bag. Your mega box of 1,000 sweetener packets is too large to fit in the sugar bag area, so your best solution was to lay it on top of the other baking supplies, except every morning something else falls over when you reach for the sweetener box. Lastly, your mugs sit with the everyday plate set since, you know, it's part of the set. Um, WWSBD? Baristas have all their core beverage making gear conveniently and efficiently stored in a single location instead of four different areas. It's time for a change in your kitchen.

Picture the potential. Take a before picture of the future barista station cupboard in all its glory, making sure to capture each shelf of the cupboard and any pantry storage near the space. Upload pictures of the spaces into a well-labeled album via a free photo and storage file sharing app, such as Dropbox™. Having before photos of your space will be valuable and motivating for you. In addition, they will be a future reference and evidence for the bragging rights you've earned once you have ignited the organizer in you.

Sketch it out. Use a traditional measuring tape to get some dimensions. Then, do a quick, rough sketch of the space and shelves. Be conservative in your findings by rounding down your numbers to the nearest 1/8 of an inch. Mark obstructions for areas you need to work around such as hinges on the cupboards. For instance, if there is an electrical panel on the pantry wall, measure where it starts and stops from all the surrounding walls (i.e., north – south – east – west).

Progress over paralysis. Don't overthink this phase. Just assess by staying focused, keeping notes, and taking measurements. This isn't an architecture class. Instead, think of it as a lower level math class where accuracy of conservative numbers is more important than fancy sketches.

How are you currently using this space? What works and what doesn't?

What are the top 5 knots that need untangling in this space? Shelves too high to reach, etc. The sugar bag makes a mess every time I use it, etc.

#1 Knot _____

#2 Knot _____

#3 Knot _____

#4 Knot _____

#5 Knot _____

What activities would you like to do in this space? Create your beverage of choice all in one spot without having to dash to four locations?

Check the condition of the space to determine if any repairs or design changes need to be made.

Doors

* **Condition:** Are any broken, need repair, or replacement?

* **Function:** Are the doors always open? Consider popping the hinged pin off and storing the door under your bed for a month or two. You often gain significant wall space behind the door and might even discover hook capabilities that were limited with the door present.

* **Style Options:** What could be changed to complete this space? Bi-fold mirror style or trendy barn-door style? Think about it!

Shelving

* **Condition:** Are there any broken shelves that need replacing? If any are a bit warped, try turning them upside down. If edges are chipped, see if you can swap out a newer looking shelf from above for one at eye level that appears worn.

* **Function:** Mark down what type of shelf you have now and how it is supported. Traditional chrome pins or clear clips typically support most shelves.

* **Style Options:** Melamine, solid wood, or floating glass are the most common shelving types. You can usually match your existing shelving with ones offered at home improvement stores. It is best to bring an existing shelf

and supporting pin with you to find the perfect match at your local home improvement store or kitchen contractor store.

Lighting

* **Condition:** Are any broken, need repair, or would be better put on a dimmer switch?
* **Function:** Would spotlights make it easier to see in this corner?
* **Style Options:** What is the vibe you are going for in the space?

Designer Eye: For a $100 consultation fee, The Container Store offers the Contained Home Program where a highly qualified closet designer and/or professional organizer provides an in-home consultation to discuss your space needs, style, and budget. They oversee your entire project from in-home consultation through the day of install.

Designers take care of all the details that go into creating your dream space by coordinating interior pictures, sketching future solutions, providing a 3D computer-assisted design of the finished project, and suggesting the perfect completion products offered for any space in your home. My team of gurus and I are proud to be the ONLY Official Brand Partner of The Container Store where we oversee all three Valley locations in Phoenix, Arizona!

Look at all your great detective work! You've taken photos and notes and have passed first base. You are ready to move into the **Attack Phase.**

ATTACK PHASE

Warning! This still is NOT "drive straight to the store or hop online in search of the right product to solve my problem right now stage," so please STOP!

STOP wasting your energy.

STOP being ineffective and unproductive.

STOP thinking your ideas will work this time or that this time will be different because it won't.

STOP running straight to third base when you haven't yet gone to second.

Instead, trust me to guide you. Together, we will ignite the organizer in you. I guarantee hands down, cross my heart over and over again until a scar is left, that you will succeed. You will gain organizing knowledge, and we will figure out what has been missing that has caused your projects to go awry.

At this point in the process, stay focused and follow the Four A's! It is more important to see and experience the progress you're making by observing and now by relying on your decision-making skills. This exercise builds your confidence. Basic practice and repetition will help rewire your brain to think and decide differently as your inner organizer ignites. Because you are changing patterns, you will alter the outcome. Remember, it is more about the next item and decision. Do this over and over (repeatedly), and new successful habits will follow.

Attack and decide what you are keeping, tossing, or donating. Above your coffee maker is a sizable cupboard with multiple adjustable shelves. Hmm. This space would be perfect for your new barista station. Remove all the items from each shelf and wipe them clean using the baby wipes from your Organizing Tool Kit. Store the holiday mugs with the appropriate seasonal décor in your garage. Donate promotional marketing mugs, unless you just happen to really love a certain design or style. Ask your spouse and other family members which their favorites are. Text a photo if they're not on hand to ask. If there are sentimental items—like a childhood mug that makes you smile but won't work in the microwave—put those into your Maybe Pile of Misfits™—you need to think about these and decide if you really, truly have to keep them. And if so, where's the best spot? Continue sorting the remainder of the cupboard inventory into appropriate piles.

Next, grab four cardboard boxes or plastic totes/tubs that you have on hand and fetch your nifty Organizing Tool Kit to the space where you are working. Label each box as follows:

* **Trash:** For food trash, wrappers, broken items, you name it. It's pure trash.
* **Recycle:** For items that you can place in your own recycling bins or bring to a recycling center.
* **Donate:** Limit your recipients to no more than two. If the volume is large and time is limited, select a company that offers pick-up service. I believe all your items have value. Do you? However, every item doesn't keep the same value to you throughout your entire life's existence.

* **Consignment/Gift:** You have packed and unpacked the same tea set repeatedly, and it still doesn't warm your heart like it used to. Better to bring a smile to another person in your community this very week! That is a gift you are giving someone by making the decision to pass on that item.

* **Maybe Pile of Misfits:** Remember the Island of Misfit Toys in the classic movie *Rudolph the Red Nose Reindeer?* No one wanted to keep or play with misfit toys, so they just stayed together, lonely and unloved. This is exactly how your items feel as they sadly sit, stored together on the floor in your guest room or garage. These misfits are starving to belong to someone and have value. Don't make the mistake of making these items misfit members for life! A dear client of mine coined this phrase about her misfit earrings, and I have used it ever since to describe this sorting theme which brings humor when deciding on the hard things.

WARNING! If you notice the Maybe Pile is changing from a pile to an island, then pause and ask yourself, "Why do I consistently store unused items for myself? Why am I robbing another from embracing and enjoying them?" If you have a compassionate, sensitive heart, does that make you feel sad? I am sure it does, especially because I know you have a heart and I know it's beating. Sometimes you just need someone, like me, to help you make healthy, quality decisions about what items you **need** to own versus **want** to own. If this didn't help you power through your maybe pile further, then tackle this pile as a smaller side project, such as one described in the Coaches Corner chapter at the end of the book. Once you have successfully completed the sorting, you are ready to begin the Assign Phase.

ASSIGN PHASE

We've made it to third base, and this time did it after passing first and second in the correct order. You've assessed your space, attacked the volume, and now you're ready to start the assign phase. At this point, you assign a final place and product for a theme—a group of like items—that can be stored in a variety of ways: on a shelf, in a drawer, in a basket, or in a lidded tote. Your final system is only assigned once you have successfully completed the Assess and Attack phases.

How to make every organizing solution P.O.P. Every organizing solution, whether big, small, or somewhere in between, must P.O.P.—it must be pretty, organized, and purposeful. Each letter of the acronym serves a purpose. If your solution does not address each letter, then you truly don't have an effective solution.

I've found this to be true with countless clients who couldn't figure out *what* piece of the solution was missing and *why* a solution didn't work. Once I explain my P.O.P. concept, they realize that they only addressed one or two of the letters instead of *all three*. While this difference seems *small*, it is incredibly *significant* on a larger scale. In order to make your solutions "pop" in color, design, budget, and family functionality, you must utilize P.O.P. This is what it must take to make *any* organizing system work *for* you and not *fight* you. Here's a more detailed explanation of P.O.P:

PRETTY: The item appeals to your personal eye and reflects your interior style as well as the design vibe you want in any given space.

ORGANIZED: The item keeps similar-themed contents corralled together, labeled accordingly, and maintainable with the future help of yourself and family or other responsible parties.

PURPOSEFUL: The item serves a true function and personal purpose for numerous reasons, otherwise it is clutter. If you don't need it, then it's another knick-knack.

An example of something that follows my P.O.P. methodology is my coffee barista station, located in our kitchen.

It is *Pretty*. Ground coffee is poured from our big Costco container into a clear acrylic OXO® container with a fresh white pop-top lid.

It is *Organized*. The coffee stays contained and fresh with a scooper sitting inside it.

It is **Purposeful**. The containers are nicely labeled for coffee and tea, so they are purposeful not only in the cupboard but handy for house guests and when entertaining.

In addition to P.O.P., your assigned system must be well labeled so all family members understand what it houses. The last thing you want is to serve regular coffee at night when guests wanted decaf. Unless you prefer for them to stay all night!

Assign the organizing system. Start the assigning process by first placing back on the shelf nonnegotiable items.

* Favorite daily mugs for at home and on-the-go.
* Tall glasses for iced tea.
* Repurpose that keepsake memory mug for housing whimsically striped paper straws.
* Add a few extra cups and glasses for visiting guests.

Now, let's add supplies as well as a system for keeping them organized. We've broken this into three budget categories, the bare-bones, moderate, and the fancy-pants budget.

Sweetener Packets

* **Bare-Bones Budget:** Dig into your Bin of Bins and use the top of a check book box or repurpose a food container.
* **Moderate Budget:** Repurpose a small ceramic container normally reserved for entertaining that will now get daily use. If you are going for the vintage vibe, then mini-glass mason jars, such as the Quattro

Stagioni® series, are darling. Use one jar to house a variety of packets or use separate jars to store brands individually and place on a decorative silver tray. If you want a timeless modern look, then the acrylic sweetener tray from InterDesign Linus® is a nice solution that offers sections to house each packet type in one slender tray.

* **Fancy-Pants Budget:** Purchase the Like-it® Brand Bricks solution offered in translucent, white or smoke. The dividers easily snap into place which nicely separates each packet type.

Regular and Decaf Coffee Storage

* **Bare-Bones Budget:** Head back to your Bin of Bins or use original coffee cans if they are not too large and awkward. You can even try to remove the label and add a more creative one to jazz up the look.

* **Moderate Budget:** Buy a unique gift item at your local gourmet food store that is filled with a product you would use regardless. Use the food inside it and repurpose the container for your barista station. You pay a tad bit more for the clever container, but you are getting double the buying power and gifting the item to yourself!

* **Fancy-Pants Budget:** Search online for styles and themes you want to complete your barista station. From casual, yet classic glass mason jars with chalkboard labels to timeless modern acrylic air tight OXO brand pop-top containers.

Regular and Decaf Coffee Pods

* **Bare-Bones Budget:** Visit your Bin of Bins or use the original containers if they are the right size for your space. Add your own labeling to jazz up the look.

* **Moderate Budget:** Buy a unique gift item in an appealing style. Use the product and repurpose the beautiful gift container or basket.

* **Fancy-Pants Budget:** For a vintage look, try Hermetic® glass storage jars. For a classic, modern look, check out Anchor Hocking® glass containers. The OXO containers are a go-to favorite of mine. They suit many styles and are made of acrylic with airtight, pop-tops. They come with either white or stainless tops. All of the above options can make every day barista stations fun, functional, personal, and easy for entertaining as well.

Tea Bag Assortments

* **Bare-Bones Budget:** Dig into your Bin of Bins or use a sharp pair of scissors and nicely cut the front or top of the box for easy access and ease in stacking your flavors.

* **Moderate Budget:** Buy a unique tea blend from your local gourmet café that comes in a stylish storage container that would nicely fit in your cupboard. It also makes an impressive statement when entertaining.

* **Fancy-Pants Budget:** Purchase an acrylic tea box that offers a variety of sections to house your tea. Place all the tea bags facing upright to complete the well-organized look.

Flavored Syrup Assortments

* **Bare-Bones Budget:** Repurpose an old salad dressing bottle by rubbing off the label and removing the sicky residue. Write on glass bottle using a Sharpie or chalk marker.

* **Moderate Budget:** Adhere a unique chalkboard label to a bottle and label by using a metallic or colored chalk pen to bring interest to your morning routine. Replace the twist-off cap with a tight rubber stopper with a chrome-tipped spout.

* **Fancy-Pants Budget:** Purchase a set of small glass bottles with chrome spout pours to house all your flavored syrup stock. Label all bottles accordingly.

ACCOUNTABLE PHASE

You've assessed, attacked, assigned, and you're almost done. This is the sweet spot reward zone—the accountable phase. You've made it safely to home plate. The hard work is behind you, and you get to reap the benefits of daily organized home living. Now, you have to commit to keeping it that way. Your hard-earned, well-organized systems can easily become dismantled in a matter of weeks. From your newfound barista station to moving toward more challenging spaces in your home—it's easy to slip. Habit, habits, habits. It may take some time to create the habit of putting everything back in its proper spot, but building this consistency and accountability brings enormous benefits. The best one? You can chill out in maintenance mode while quickly making a cup of coffee. It is rare for clients to allow their newly organized spaces to return to their original condition, so don't ruin our record and be that anomaly!

Labeling is lovely on many levels. Double-check that everything around your barista station is well labeled. Labeling does the speaking for you. Imagine never being asked again for the rest of your life mundane questions like, "Is this the regular coffee or the decaf?" A label could have answered this question for you. If someone asks me a question that is easily answered by reading the labels, I count in my head 1 … 2 … 3 … and then hear, "Oh, there it is! Thanks, Danielle!"

Give your loved ones a grand tour of the newly organized space. Select a time to show and fully explain every item on every shelf of your new barista station. Like a game show, test their knowledge: Devon, where are the sugar packets? Oliver, where are the tea bags kept? Yes, it seems hokey, and your family will think you have lost your marbles organizing. However, this act of explaining the system to everyone who will use it is a true nonnegotiable. Skipping this step is what causes breakdowns during the accountability phase and results in some clients giving up.

Another reason this tour is so important is because the system can't work for only you; it must work for your entire household. For instance, my hubby bought a big tub of coconut oil that he wanted to use in the coffee area, but he thought it was too big and clumsy. I poured the liquid into a glass bottle with a chrome spout, added a chalk label, and promptly created a solution. The bottle stands on the counter beside the coffee maker. I listened to his needs and devised a plan. That is what organizing is all about.

Time to work the system. For the next few days, notice if your newly organized barista station works. What items need tweaking? Shelf adjustments so you can reach items? Any products or placement of your inventory that seems to be missing? Just like products in today's marketplace go through an intense series of testing prior to being sold, so should your organizing system. The more open-minded and adaptable you are, the more successful your system will be in serving your household and the more likely it will be that your family members will help maintain it.

Hi-yah to you for kicking ace in learning the 4 A's of organizing!

 You have earned another bundle of kindling to keep your organizing flame burning within if you successfully completed the following:

❑ You wrote a new playbook for organizing by understanding the 4 A's to follow: Assess, Attack, Assign, and Accountable.

Assess Phase

❑ You conquered Progress over Paralysis.
❑ You checked the space to determine if any repairs or changes need to be made.

Attack Phase

❑ You Asked Yourself What Would a Starbucks Barista Do? (WWSBD)

- ❑ You applied your skills by creating your own barista coffee or tea station.
- ❑ You attacked all inventory deciding what to keep, toss, donate, consign/gift, or place in a maybe pile.

Assign Phase

- ❑ You learned about and how to make every organizing solution P.O.P.
- ❑ You learned how to Assign an organizing system from the barista station example—e.g., Sweetener Packets, Coffee Pods, Tea Bag Assortments, and Flavored Syrup Assortments.

Accountable Phase

- ❑ You experienced how lovely labeling is by testing it out on your label maker machine.
- ❑ You've given the grand tour of the newly organized space to your loved ones.

Congratulations! You have learned the Four A's and successfully used them to create for yourself a well-organized barista station. Successfully completing this small project has proven your skills as an organizer. You know that with every organizing project you assess, attack, assign, and stay accountable. The order in which you approach a project stays the same and it gives you the power to be successful in every situation—big or small. Let's move on to the next part of the book as we begin using the Four A's in different spaces throughout your home.

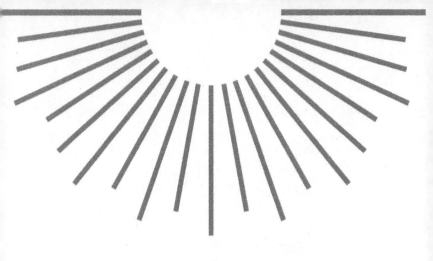

MATTERS
— OF THE —
HANDS

CLOSETS AND BEDROOMS: FROM SHUTTING THE DOOR TO LEAVING IT OPEN

Now that you have mastered the Four A's of organizing, it is time to consolidate and fully ignite all your organizing skills, from gatekeeping and decision-making to assessing and attacking. Bedrooms and closets are notorious for being the place where personal items throughout the house get deposited when guests are arriving. No one will look in there, right? The bedroom is the most sacred and intimate space in the home. It is where we rise each morning refreshed and lay our heads in the evening to recharge our minds and bodies. If your bedroom isn't offering you and your life mate a healthy, restful environment, then eventually your inner battery will die, and you will need jumper cables to revive it.

What is Your Wardrobe and Body Relationship?

Closet organization projects can initially be tough because there is a strong emotional and psychological connection between you, your belongings, and your current space. This relationship can be healthy, toxic, or somewhere wedged in between. Assessing your wardrobe, how it reflects the current you, and determining what clothing to keep and what to donate is a large part of organizing a closet.

Do you know your body's natural assets and liabilities? Do you know how to accentuate the positive? If not, quickly do some research and get those questions resolved. When determining which clothing and accessories to retain, you want to be sure they are flattering on you and still fashionable.

Colors That Complement

Do you know which colors reflect best on your skin tone? I once attended a color draping workshop that revealed jewel tones work best for my Italian olive skin, particularly every possible shade of purple.

Shortly after I had my first son, my mom took me to the Chanel lipstick counter where a make-up consultant matched me with what seemed to be a bright, vampire-red lip color. For cryin' out loud, I was pushing a baby stroller, not biting necks for blood at midnight! However, my sophisticated Manhattan Italian mother is always right. Although brutally honest when advising my sister and me on beauty- and fashion-related tips, she would never steer us wrong—never! When she said, "Danielle, now *that* color literally makes your *entire* face light up!" and the counter consultant quickly chimed in agreement, I trusted the experts and went ahead with the $50 investment for the vampire purchase. Since then, I receive at least five compliments on the days I wear that darn "vampy" Chanel red lipstick. It is quite humorous and predictable. When selecting your style colors, focus on quality and hues that compliment you best ... then ditch the rest!

ASSESS PHASE

Since a closet space requires more in-depth direction, I thought it would be best to focus on closet details first. I will address the bedroom space a bit later in the chapter. Let's now review the closet including the condition of doors, lighting, and shelving, with an investigative eye as we learned to do in earlier chapters. The following categories are areas that typically need to be assessed in closets:

Assess the space and its function. How does the space feel to you? Does it work? Is space being utilized fully? Which area needs further analysis?

Picture the potential. What did the before photographs reveal to you? Are there areas that you want to change? Areas that you like?

Sketch it out. Measure and outline all areas of the closet, including doors, shelf spacing, electrical outlets, and any architectural features, such arches or windows.

Progress over paralysis. You've got this! It's just like the barista station, only on a larger scale. Let's get started.

How are you currently using this space? What works and what doesn't?

What are the top 5 knots that need untangling in this space? Long hanging clothes hitting the floor? Not enough shelves? Need drawers or hooks for accessories? Where to put shoes?

What activities would you like to do in this space? Get dressed, relax, listen to music, or a podcast? Read? Watch a movie?

Check the condition of the space to determine if any repairs or structural/design changes need to be made. Place an X where you need to repair or reconsider your current setup. Go to chapter 6 for more details on what steps you can take here.

Doors:	__ Condition	__ Function	__ Style Options
Shelves:	__ Condition	__ Function	__ Style Options
Lighting:	__ Condition	__ Function	__ Style Options

You've thoroughly assessed the space so you're now ready for the next phase—attack!

ATTACK PHASE

Before beginning to attack, let's think about what you wear and how you want to look. Clothing reflects your personality, so it's important to keep items that suit you and make you happy. Recognizing what looks good on you and what items you really love allows you use your decision-making skills to decide which of your dearly loved clothing you will keep and which you will donate, so others can share the joy of what you let go.

Remember: you want to keep those belongings that enhance your looks and confidence. The following suggestions should help guide the process.

Everything Has Value

I have yet to meet someone who doesn't believe all things in this world have value to someone, somewhere in some way. However, it does *not* mean they *all* need to have value to *you*. Throughout the book, I talk about visualizing someone else enjoying your treasure rather than having it collect dust and take up space in your home.

If you don't readily use something, then it is clutter. No, don't try to justify it. It IS clutter. Let it find a second life with someone else!

Frameworks

I find that giving clients a framework works incredibly well when it's time to exercise and expedite a closet decision-making experience. This framework gives my clients both the freedom to make decisions and set boundaries within which to work. The system allows you to embrace who you are and focuses you on the clothes that you truly want and need to store. I have developed two sorting methodologies: *The Clutter-Free Cruise Approach* and *The Magical Measurement Method.*

The Clutter-Free Cruise Approach

Imagine you are living luxuriously onboard a cruise ship. This majestic ship holds your entire clothing wardrobe. The captain of the ship frantically announces that this grand ship is overburdened with too much weight and that everyone must limit their luggage. Time to begin selecting your *Savvy 75 Survival* pieces (aka, S.S.S.). These are the items that you keep to survive the cruise, while ditching the rest to reduce the ship's weight and keep the boat afloat. Yes, I know this scenario sounds ridiculously dramatic. Your life, and not your wardrobe, is in jeopardy, but hey, it makes the decision-making exercise process in this chapter way more fun, right? Totally!

Magical Measurement Method

Measure your linear hanging space using your contractor's tape from your tool kit. Every 1 inch of linear space is equivalent to 1 stored item. For example, 60 inches of upper short hang and 60 inches for lower long hang equals 120 inches of linear space to store a maximum of 120 items. The M.M.M. is also easy-peasy decision making, right?

Choosing Your Essential Pieces

Now that you've selected your sorting method ... start with your nonnegotiable themes!

Set a timer on your phone for 30 minutes and start diving in to find the pieces that most reflect your core personality, fashion sense, and current lifestyle. Undergarments, support wear, swimwear, layering pieces, and heavy outer coats *do not apply* in the count for either **S.S.S. or M.M.M.** Neither do accessories such as purses, crossbody bags, boots, or shoes.

I suggest looking at all the pieces of a single theme at once (for instance, all long pants or work blouses). Once you have collected the themed pile, select your *most* favorite items down to your *least* favorite. Lay each theme pile neatly on your bed so you can add or delete pieces. If an item is in the laundry or at the dry cleaner, then jot its name down on a single piece of bright colored paper from your Organizing Tool Kit as a reminder to pack it for your survival on the boat trip ahead.

For my own Clutter-Free Cruise packing experience I selected the following:

- ✳ 12 rompers and/or dresses (it's an insta-outfit!)
- ✳ 8 vests and/or outfit jackets (I cringe at being cold)
- ✳ 10 T-shirts (short sleeve) and 10 (long sleeve)
- ✳ 5 casual shorts and 5 casual skirts
- ✳ 5 workout tops and 5 workout bottoms
- ✳ 3 soccer mom fan favorites
- ✳ 10 dressy tops and 5 casual bottoms
- ✳ 2 dress pants. (I don't look good in pants. So, if the ship goes down and I don't have room to pack pants, I would survive just fine in my new life.)

If the Clutter-Free Cruise Method stresses you out or you have a generous amount of storage options in your residence, then you may prefer using my M.M.M instead.

Maybe Pile of Misfits

The big question now is how to handle the balance of your inventory, that infamous Maybe Pile of Misfits. The timer has now gone off, and hopefully, you have selected your S.S.S. or M.M.M. pieces. Now, you look around at what's left and wonder what to do with the inventory volume in your Misfit Pile and ponder the financial investment spent on the items that didn't make the cut! Wow! You have made it this far! Don't feel discouraged. Also, avoid the temptation to grab items from the Misfit Pile. You'll only sink the ship with your overpacking or cram your closet full of items that won't actually fit anymore.

Instead, take a deep breath. I am right by your side, and I am now throwing you an arsenal of options. Stay focused and dive back into your Organizing Tool Kit. Grab six bright pieces of paper and write the following six subcategories in large font with a Sharpie BEFORE you power through the balance of your Maybe Pile of Misfits.

First, do not force yourself to decide unless you are 150 percent positive that the item in question should be placed in a particular theme pile. Any doubt in your decision-making skills decreases your inner organizer mojo and gravely slows progress. Go forth, my friend, and listen to what your head and your heart is telling you, so your hands can do the work.

Your outstanding Maybe Pile of Misfits will likely fall into the following six categories:

1. **"I could fit back into this, but it will take me <u>under</u> a year to lose the weight" pieces.** It's life vest time! Strap it on, and you now need to make some tougher decisions: In order to keep an item, you must truly, deeply, and honestly be committed to losing the appropriate weight. Also, the color and style need to be current and complimentary.

2. **"It will take me <u>over</u> a year to lose the weight" pieces.** Are you ready to commit to a liquid diet for the next 12 months? Are you willing to quit drinking soda, processed foods, and instead start eating fresh, healthy real food? If you go gluten free, corn free, sugar free and break a sweat in any form of random exercise five times a week, then your system will be jump-started for significant change. This is what it will take to shed some serious weight, and you must be willing to store excess inventory for the next two years. Realize fashion styles change, your taste may change, and your body shape is likely to change. Frankly, it serves no purpose to play the storage game. It's better to release the guilt, consign the pieces, enjoy the store credit or extra cash on hand, AND indulge in the open closet space you've granted yourself.

3. **Worth your valuable time to mend yourself or worth your wallet monies and precious free time to drive to the alteration shop and pay someone to mend it for you.** Regardless of the items you place in this theme pile, the cost better be seriously worth it! This pile has dollar signs written all over it. Save yourself the time and money investment, forgive yourself the guilt, and move onto the next theme pile.

4. **Future consignment or private posting.** Only create this pile if you will shop at a consignment store or if you are committed to taking photos and posting online via apps such as OfferUp® or LetGo®. Is it worth your time? If none of these option interests you, then simply skip this theme pile.

5. **Donatable goods for another's life.** My favorite donation story is when I helped a client reorganize her pantry. She had a $300, brand-new, high-end juicing machine that sat high on her pantry shelf processing only dust. I guaranteed her that there was someone out there who would benefit from the appliance, and she agreed. We placed it aside in her donation pile. One week later, my client was at a MOPS meeting at our church, and the ladies were going around the table sharing their prayer requests. One mom was recently diagnosed with a rare cancer, and her request was for the financial resources to purchase that exact juicing machine! Both girls were strangers and neither knew that I knew them both and their current situations. Through my client's giving heart and organizing project, she was able to help the mom with cancer. God connected them through the juicer, which was exchanged shortly after the meeting. True story! How could I possibly make this up, right?

Other easily donatable items are kids' clothes. I typically pass some of my boy's outgrown clothes on to a friend and the rest goes to a local charity or two where I can conveniently drop off items. If you're a Pinterest Perfectionist personality, be careful not to become a part-time Uber driver where you are dropping off goods to more than two or three resources. It's better to pass along items within the week than have them sit in shopping bags for months.

Powerhouse donation stores like Goodwill® or Savers® partner with many local charities. So, when their inventory runs high, they can pass goods along and continue to provide value to these other local organizations. Damaged textiles are compacted and shipped to countries to be repurposed into woven goods for clothing, baskets, or blankets.

Convinced now where some of your "maybe pile" items can go? Hope so! Don't overthink the resources, just grab a few colored sheets, take a moment to mark in Sharpie your donation resources on a few hearty-handled shopping bags.

6. **Memory pieces.** I stored my bulky keepsake college sweatshirt in my memory bin for more than 20 years, and recently, I decided to pass it along. The son of a soccer mom that I know was attending my alma mater and loved retro-style clothing. I surprised them with the sweatshirt. Since then, their family loves telling me how their son says it is his favorite piece of clothing.

If I didn't have that immediate connection with this family, then parting with the sweatshirt would have gone differently. I would probably have either taken a silly selfie in the sweatshirt or with my kiddos wearing it. I would then have taken a close-up image of the shirt, printed a color copy, and placed the photo in a clear protective sleeve to be stored in my personal memory box. Sometimes it is more important to give items a second life rather than rob another person of the experience to appreciate owning it. Select the absolute, bottom-line, bare bones memory pieces and then put the rest aside in your Maybe Pile of Misfits.

What if I still have items (and I mean a lot of items) leftover? What pile do they go into?

You likely are physically and mentally depleted at this point. It's best not to force yourself into making rash decisions until your mind is fresh again. Look how far you have come! Look how much you accomplished! You are an on-fire organizing rock star. As far as storing items not yet reviewed, here's how to handle it:

1) Place a dark garbage bag over hangered items so you won't feel overwhelmed seeing the remaining balance. If you find you are not searching for certain pieces, then **there's** your sign!

2) Toss loose clothes in one shopping bag and loose shoes/ purses in a separate one.

3) It will be more manageable to review the balance of your inventory from both a time and inventory perspective if they are separated out.

Jot down a future shopping list. Notice holes in your wardrobe? Literally and figuratively? See a shirt with armpit stains or holes worn in it? Note that item on a future shopping list. You could even apply consignment income to purchase the item. Consider treating yourself to a new piece of clothing once you successfully complete a certain step in your organization process. You will feel so confident when wearing it knowing what it took to truly earn its reward.

ASSIGN PHASE

We don't realize how many different types of clothes and items we store until we make an itemized inventory of it all. It seems daunting, but I know it will dazzle you once it's complete. I know it sounds cliché to say just "trust me in the process" and that it won't be as painful as you think, but it's true and more rewarding than you realize.

Return items back in color order. It has been psychologically and scientifically proven that we dress according to our mood. I persuasively suggest arranging your closet to enhance you daily mood and ease of dressing. Do you know Roy G. Biv? The letters of this fictional name are an acronym for the sequence of hues that are reflected in a conventional rainbow: red, orange, yellow, green, blue, indigo, and violet = ROYGBIV. Extend that rainbow sequence to accommodate the other colors that are reflected in your wardrobe. It might look something like this: white, cream, ROGBI, pink, V, taupe, dark brown, gray, and black. You decide what rainbow of color order is right for you. In the end, your righteous rainbow will be yours—personal, beautiful, and orderly to your eye, which is what matters most.

File your clothes in a fashionable order. Much like properly filing papers in an office, your clothes need to be placed in their proper clothing theme order. You wouldn't haphazardly shove your bank statements into randomly themed folders, so why would you file your clothes back in the same fashion? Get it ... fashion? Clothes? LOL. So, to kick off the assignment process, I tape a colored 3x5 index card to the garment bar of the closet section or hole punch the card and place over the first hanger item that represents that theme. Start placing the nonnegotiable hanger items back first, filing them from left to right in theme order, then size, then solid color, then pattern. For example, you would arrange short sleeve polo shirts in white, red, red striped, yellow, light blue, dark blue, taupe, and black. Once all short sleeve polos have been placed in the tagged polo section, then move on to marking the themed label for long sleeve polos shirts. File your hanger theme items beginning with the top nonnegotiable order for items that need to be hung. Place your more frequently worn themed items at your fingertips and less frequent items in less accessible locations. See my suggested order and list below to review before you proceed assigning a system.

On-the-Hanger Themes

* **Tops:** blouses, button-down shirts, polo shirts, vests, tanks, and tees
* **Bottoms:** dress pants, casual pants, and jeans
* **Suits:** Suit Sets
* **Long Hang:** tunics, short dresses, long dresses*
* **Dresses:** If your closet doesn't offer a long hang section, then convert your long hang item to short hang by folding the long hang over a pant hanger, therefore cutting the length of that piece in half.
* **Jackets:** dressy blazers, casual blazers, and jackets
* **Outerwear:** vests, outer jackets, and coats
* **Special Occasion Items:** gowns, tuxedos
* **Knits:** vests, button-up cardigans, sweaters, and sweatshirts

- * **Athletic Gear:** tops, bottoms, supportive, gear-related accessories
- * **Uniforms and Cheer Gear:** scrubs, work/promo clothing, and sports-related items
- * **Accessories:** ties, belts, and scarves

Hangers

When in the assigning phase for a closet, it's important to discuss hangers. For Wurth Organizing, having all the same color and style hanger in a closet is a flat-out nonnegotiable. Don't try to convince me or yourself otherwise! It's like wearing a snazzy outfit with two types of shoes … it looks odd because it is odd. Your closet will visually transform from crappy to classy in under an hour.

Before going out to buy new hangers, look to see which color and style hangers you currently own. If you see mostly white tubular, and you like it and it fits your budget, then add to your current white tubular theme. You can remove other colored hangers and make that color and style the consistent closet theme for another space.

Also note that hanger styles must be easy for you to reset and remove clothes on a daily basis. If certain styles are too frustrating on your fingers due to physical limitations, then it's best to bring a few clothing items into the store to properly select the right style of hanger that fits your personal needs.

Also, take a moment to refer to the before image of your space. Notice what hangers look cohesive in style and which ones stick out.

Bare-Bones Budget: Swap out as many hangers as possible of one color or style from other closet locations to keep hanger consistency within each closet.

Moderate Budget: Plastic tubular hangers run about 10 cents each and come in a variety of fun vibrant colors to give your wardrobe a fun pop of style! They also are offered in bulk at most thrift stores.

Fancy-Pants Budget: Slimline velvet hangers from inventor Joy Mangano® run about $1 dollar per hanger. However, their design saves significant space and prevents future damaging of your items because it stops them from easily slipping onto the floor. For skirt and suit sets only, I prefer using the classic crystal retail style hangers that offer hearty chrome clips, so I can triple up my hanging space per hanger.

Go to **WurthOrganizing.com** where you'll find **My 100-Item: Wardrobe Wonderlist** and **Clothing Theme Tag Printable** so it will be on hand to take note of your potential shopping list needs. Before starting the Assign Phase, make sure you've successfully completed the Attack Phase and tallied your needs. This form of self-control only comes through practice and experience. Be wise and not wasteful of what you have been given.

On-the-Shelf or In-a-Drawer

Shelf or drawer space should house clothing you do not have the square footage to hang in a closet or items that you just *prefer* to store folded. Refer to your clothing theme list and see which themes would be best folded and stored on shelves or in drawers. Place your more frequently used themed items on shelves located at your fingertip height and less frequently used items in less accessible shelf locations. Fold and file back each theme just like you did for the hangered items. Place back your top nonnegotiable items first in the color order of your choosing.

Because this theme of items was not included in the Attack Phase of selecting your keeper pieces for your Clutter Free Cruise or Magical Measurement Method, now is the time to truly review the remaining inventory of personal items stored in your closet.

Fear of Folding

It takes literally 3 seconds—1 Mississippi … 2 Mississippi … 3 Mississippi … no big deal!

Practice a few ways to fold that work for you and fit your shelf location best. Always keep the finished edge facing forward because it looks cleaner to the eye and makes it easier to tell between one shirt and another when stacked. If you are a smaller frame person then fold the item once vertically, then in half. If you are a larger frame person then tri-fold the item vertically folding the arms and side back and then fold up the bottom once, if not twice to get a finished edge. In drawers, I suggest placing the finished edge facing up, I call it *bookend-style*, much like the spine of a book facing you. Again, I highly suggest folding 'n' filing back in color order. Bottom line, pick a folding style that fits the space and your preference.

Now that you are left with the final, final balance of your personal inventory, grab the coordinating **Clothing Theme Tags** and place them on the spot where the items will be stored. See additional Accessories Themes below. Fold, file, and store in your righteous rainbow order:

- ✳ Short sleeve T-shirts
- ✳ Long sleeve T-shirts
- ✳ Purses
- ✳ Shoes
- ✳ Athletic shoes
- ✳ Boots
- ✳ Sports bags
- ✳ Travel bags

If your closet doesn't offer any sections for folded items, then you can easily create one:

Bare Bones Budget: Divide your shelving area into sections by sliding a chrome or acrylic shelf divider onto a shelf. They create a nice divider for folded themes and prevent stacks from falling like a Jenga Tower. I prefer a tight mesh metal pattern or the solid acrylic style which prevents clothes from poking thru the dividers. They can easily be moved as your inventory changes and are very wallet friendly, ranging from only $4 - 7 each.

Moderate Budget: If you don't have a shelf or prefer another storage style option, then you can screw or bolt a decorative bin or basket directly onto an open wall area of your closet.

Select a style option that speaks to you—from painted wood to woven wicker or wire mesh-style baskets. Make sure the finish of the product doesn't wear off or snag your folded clothing when stored. Pricing can range from $15–$25 per bin or basket depending on your selection.

Fancy-Pants Budget: Purchase a mesh Elfa® Start-A-Stack mesh drawer system from The Container Store. It supplies a generous amount of storage for the space with clear visibility into each drawer. The mesh drawers are offered in 1, 2, or 3 runner depths and offer tremendous flexibility so you can decide how you want to place your drawers on the supportive tracks. Pricing for the stack system depends on which drawer depth you prefer and can run from $50—$200 per stack system. If you desire a more sophisticated built-in solution entirely, then consider the Avera or Laren closet line options also offered through The Container Store.

Clean, Preserve, and Protect

As you sort your inventory into its appropriate clothing or accessory themes, take a moment to clean and tidy. Use baby wipes to remove harmful dust off all new or existing shelves, shoes, boots, purses, etc. Use leather wipes or a few drops of olive oil to preserve all leather-like materials because they are a living fabric that needs to breathe. Inspect all items for damage and make note on your **Wardrobe Wonderlist** the tasks that are required to repair or maintain specific items. Next, start placing back the items that will be folded and stored on a shelf or in your Elfa Start-A-Stack.

ACCOUNTABLE PHASE

You have already completed the most painful and difficult part of this chapter! Now, we can just move into what we call Maintenance Mode, or The Sweet Spot. Only you (not me) can prevent this sweet spot from turning sour. Here are a few areas to be mindful of as you move forward on a daily basis:

Keep the floor clear at all costs: Avoid tripping hazards and keep the dust bunny brigade from shopping bags, shoes, and shipment boxes. When unpacking a new purchase, try it on and promptly decide to keep or return.

Action Step: For items you are keeping, immediately cut the tag, fold or file it away, and store receipt accordingly. You are 1,000 times more likely to wear something with tags removed—it confirms your commitment to the item and that it is a true keeper. For returns, round up all materials required in a *one-minute rule* and place in a designated area, such as office or laundry room, to wrap up within the week.

Put your dirty laundry in the hamper: Another simple task to execute daily, but unfortunately too many fail to complete successfully. We sadly see depression setting in from the vast volume of clothing spread all over the furniture and floor.

Action Step: Make sure you have an ample-size dirty clothes hamper (or more) to house your light and dark clothes. If not, purchase a matching set or double hamper system. Based on your space plan, place them either in your closet or bathroom. For dry cleaning, consider using a hearty upright handled beach bag as opposed to a drawstring bag. Drawstring bags are odd to store and awkward to lug for drop off. Conveniently place the upright bag on a hook or shelf in your closet with any coupons to redeem.

Designate an area for donations, consignments, and/or gifts: There will always be change, flow, and rotation required in your closet from one season to the next. Consistency as you rotate and remove items is important part of staying accountable.

Action Step: If your closet offers the space, then hang the appropriate Clothing Theme Tags around the items for removal or place in a protective zippered garment bag to visually eliminate the daily distraction. Even though my closet is small, I prefer to place these themes in my garage. Donates are placed in a designated bag and consigns are hung in a garment bag near the consignment tote which makes for easy transferring. Hand-me-down gifts are put in my car for quick drops to moms at school.

The easier and more repeatable you make decisions, the less likely you are to have organizing relapse. Let me repeat that again ... more repeat = less relapse. I should create my own bumper sticker with this phrase.

Happy dancing like nobody's watching now! This chapter was a mighty monster to take down ... it was a beast for me to write the darn thing, so know it was equally tough for you process it.

How to Avoid the Bedroom Blues

Make your bed every day. This is sooooo not a big deal, people, so don't attempt to turn it into one. Because your bed is the largest square footage of visible space in your bedroom, it makes the greatest visual impact. It also emotionally sets the tone for a well-organized space. Keep doing it to foster this habit on a daily basis. Don't you think a 60-second task that offers such massive benefits is worth executing? No doubt.

- **Action step:** Fold the sheet up, pull the comforter over, and then toss the pillows on top ... nothing HGTV photo fancy, just done. Completing this basic task does wonders in preventing an organizing relapse, so you won't have to go back and re-read this entire book, AGAIN, unless you want to because you missed our time together.

Remove unnecessary furniture. The more surface space you offer, the more tempted you will be to place things on a side chair, table, etc., "just for a minute." We commonly convince ourselves that it will be put away, but we know this sales pitch fails phenomenally every time. For example, you wore something for just a few hours, tossed it on a chair (which remains dusty because you never sit in it), so the outfit is not technically dirty.

- **Action Step:** Remove the dusty chair for a week to see if it is gravely missed. Select one core spot on a shelf or back door hook to place that outfit to be worn again within that week. If not worn, it gets restored to the closet or drawer at the end of the day. The more often you make these quick decisions, the less daunting staying accountable will be.

You have earned another bundle of kindling to keep your organizing flame burning within if you successfully completed the following:

Assess Phase

- ❏ You identified your body's natural born assets and liabilities and know how they relate to the categories of fit, figure, and fashion.
- ❏ The colors that complement you best have been identified and used to guide you.
- ❏ You've carefully examined, measured, and sketched your space and listed the top 5 knots to untangle.

Attack Phase

- ❏ You've decided whether the Clutter-Free Cruise or the Magical Measurement Method approach best reflects your sorting style.
- ❏ All items in your nonnegotiable themes have been completely reviewed, tallied, and accounted for selecting the essential pieces required in building your ultimate wardrobe.
- ❏ All items in your Maybe Pile of Misfits have been gone through once again so that you feel you have emotionally and physically made the best possible decisions and know that you will need to eventually eliminate this pile.
- ❏ All donatable goods have been dropped off and/or picked up.

- ❑ All consignment and/or private postings have been dropped off and/or picked up if this option is of interest to you.
- ❑ You have created a "Future Shopping List" for items that need (not want) to be purchased so you can further maximize your wardrobe.

Assign Phase

- ❑ You have put back clothing in color order and/or fashionable order so getting dressed in the morning runs seamlessly.
- ❑ All your On-the-Hanger and On-the-Shelf themes have been neatly folded and placed accordingly.

Accountable Phase

- ❑ In the closets, you have an appropriately sized hamper to house white and dark clothes. In addition, you have diligently placed your laundry directly in the hamper.
- ❑ A handled bag has been designated for future dry cleaning.
- ❑ Locations have been also assigned for donates, consigns, and gifts.
- ❑ In the bedroom, you have consistently made your bed for a week…nice work and looks great too, I bet!
- ❑ Unnecessary furniture has been removed, repurposed, sold or donated.

Congratulations! You successfully applied the Four A's to one of the toughest, but most satisfying organization projects—closets! Let's move on and apply your skills to our next organizing challenge.

8

SHOVE OUT THE SHAME
AND DRIVE IN YOUR CAR

"My front door greets my guests, but my garage door greets my family."

After a bustling day of work, school, or sports, my well-labeled and colorful garage totes softly say "welcome home" versus screaming at me in a disappointing, disorganized tone. Our garages may contain anything from sports equipment and laundry to household items and tools. My garage has cases of organizing products for my team and client workshops. Every item belongs to a **theme** (like things together, the same as in our closets) and is stored in a well-labeled **zone**. All household members know each zone's exact **location**.

Although the garage is the toughest, dirtiest, and most challenging space to tackle, it is my *personal favorite* to organize! I experience the greatest rewards with organized garage spaces giving me daily hugs back in gratitude. This is what I want your garage to give back to you, and I know it will. Not convinced? I am not asking you to learn Mandarin. I am, however, asking you to ignite the organizer within while I take your *mental* concerns and put them into *motion*.

"I _need_ to start; _I don't want_ to start, yet I _must_ start. However, I don't think I _can_ start." Does your garage look like a modern-day urban jungle? Most people are not over-the-moon-excited to spend their time off transforming their cluttered garage. I am a rare breed who views this experience differently, which is why you're reading *my* book, so I can lead *you* to the finish line. It does require some bare-bones bravery to rip off the Band-Aid and roll up the garage door, revealing the ugliness within.

Don't let temporary embarrassment rob you of the potential bragging rights in your home and your hood. If that isn't enough, then the words water leak and rats should be your motivation for sorting your precious belongings before water or rodents move in, therefore your items will be going straight to the dump! Take control now before you lose them for it is only a matter of time before someone or something will take the lead *for* you. Your efforts are likely to inspire others to spring into action, so let's get started assessing your situation.

ASSESS PHASE

Different needs and objects compete for every sliver of square footage available in a garage. Eventually, the car gets knocked out and is forced to reside in the driveway. An expensive asset now sits in the elements and not inside in its own designated space. Clearly, we have a serious priority problem that needs a resolution, which is why you are reading this chapter and taking copious notes … right?

Assess the space and its function. How does the space feel to you? Which areas need further analyzing to address?

Picture the potential. Just like any interior space, you must have a 360-degree view with all the walls in your photos. For separate parking bays, take pictures of each wall for each bay. Also snap a picture of your handyman bench or laundry area, if it applies.

What do the photographs and clues you have gathered reveal to you? What do they say about you? Having a visual reference of the shape and size of your items is so important when you get to the Assign Phase and head out shopping. (No, we're not there yet so don't even think about shopping). See an item at the store, online, or in a magazine? Take a picture of it and its barcode to help you recall its source and upload for reference.

Sketch it out. Make sure you mark all areas of all the bays from floor to ceiling.

Progress over paralysis. I know it feels like you're tackling a beast in an urban jungle, but you have got this Assess phase. Tear into it like a roaring lion, hunting and hungry.

How are you currently using this space? Ask your family what works for them and what doesn't? What's their wish list. Whose car needs to be stored in which bay due to door swing or an electric car charging station? Everyone will greatly appreciate that you're taking time to listen to their frustrations and their nonnegotiables.

What are the top 5 knots that need untangling in this space?
Bikes need to be safely rolled into racks, rather than on the floor, to avoid tripping? Where is the exit door? Where do trash/recycle bins need to be stored?

What activities would you like to do in this space? Do you like to tinker, build, and create projects? Are you sporty? Do you like to soak up the sun and fun in the fresh outdoors?

Check the condition of the space to determine if any repairs or structural/design changes need to be made. Place an X where you need to repair or reconsider your current setup. Go to chapter 6 for more details on what steps you can take here.

Doors:	__ Condition	__ Function	
Shelves:	__ Condition	__ Function	
Lighting:	__ Condition	__ Function	
Style:	__ Condition	__ Function	

ATTACK PHASE

The garage is THE ONLY space in your entire residence where everyone's personal belongings—as well as household items (cleaners, lightbulbs, A/C filters)—must reside together somehow and some way. Every item wants its space, and the garage is the ultimate square-footage slugfest! The car wants a bay to park in, the house supplies want a shelf to sit on, the tools want a utility board to hang on, the kids want a bike rack, and the dog wants a bin for its toys. Sheesh! We didn't even get to talk about what you and your spouse want.

Okay, roll up your sleeves and reveal the power of your Organizing Tool Kit. To take down this beast of a space, you must have a fully stocked and designated Organizing Tool Kit. An insane amount—and I mean a truly i-n-s-a-n-e amount, of your precious energy and daily clock time will be robbed if you are not prepared. Don't bother being stubborn on this important step. It will only derail your efforts. Diving into a garage that has a gazillion pieces and a gazillion themes without supplies at your fingertips means you will be wasting time sorting like an amateur when you are a pro. I believe you are smart, so please look smart and act smart by following my lead.

Reach for my **Geared Up Garage Checklist,** clear packing tape, and be ready to write and place Mega Zone signs on the wall to show potential storage locations. Then, you will tape the respective Minor Zones on potential boxes/bins/totes within it. This will give you a visual map of how your garage will eventually be organized.

Time to bust into your Bin of Bins. This is where you will really embrace the beauty of having your own Bins of Bins section in your home. If you elected to be a renegade and go rogue by skipping this action step earlier, you now must STOP and get it done. Quickly do a scavenger hunt gathering up your unused bins, baskets, banker boxes, and other plastic totes to use while temporarily sorting your Mega Zones and the Minor Zones that lie within each. Why?

* Because ... I said so!
* Because ... I said so! A second time in case you didn't agree with me the first time!

* The shapes and sizes of items you need to organize are limitless (from tiny screws to suitcases) so having an array of bins is the best solution.

* Labeling as you go allows you to start and stop working on the space (within reason!).

* Anyone, anytime can find anything in their temporarily labeled bin/box.

We can and will upgrade to a different more cohesive product later if desired.

Remember … progress, not perfection. Progress, not perfection. Now you got it!

To attack the garage, you first have to get all like items together in one place. At one client's home, for example, there were tools in the storage shed, kitchen junk drawer, laundry room, vehicles, and in the garage! Nothing could ever be found when needed. The same goes for multiple other garage themes. The idea is to sort EVERYTHING into its own Mega Zone and then into smaller related Minor Zones.

NOTE: If your current garage doesn't offer enough open space to effectively work, then you may need to expand your organizing operation onto the driveway. Be prepared for drive by offers from others thinking it's a garage sale so keep a watchful eye!

Identify Garage Zones

Start this process by using your Garage Printable to designate your garage's Top 8 Mega Zones (sorted alphabetically) and the smaller Minor Zones that lie within each:

Clubs and Hobbies

Minor zones include:

- ✳ Do-it-Yourself Tools of the Trade and related gear divided for each family member's related hobby, from woodworking to car enthusiasts.
- ✳ Boy Scouts / Girl Scouts – uniforms, marketing, promotion materials
- ✳ Military Related – uniforms, tactical gear

Entertainment

Minor zones include:

- ✳ Serving pieces, drink dispensers, tablecloths, cutlery, decor

Holiday Decor

Sort decor in calendar-year order. For smaller holidays (where the inventory is lower than others), consider combining two into one box, especially if they fall close together on the calendar. For example, I have one storage bin that houses Valentine's Day and Fourth of July. If Easter decor didn't take up its own 18-gallon tote, then I would have combined it with Valentine's Day because they fall close together on the calendar.

Household Items

Think of this zone in terms of aisles in a hardware store. This will visually kick-start how these Minor Zones breakdown seamlessly:

- A/C support
- Car washing
- Cleaning (surface, fabric, and floors)
- Electrical
- Gardening tools - handheld (small, large, and power tools),
- Tool parts (nuts, bolts, accessories)
- Hardware and spare parts
- Lightbulbs – indoor bulbs and outdoor bulbs
- Painting – touch-up cans, sprays, brushes, pans, and supportive gear
- Pest control
- Plumbing
- Pool related – chemicals and tester kits
- Tools - handheld (small, large, and power tools)

Memory Keepsakes

Think of this zone as that protective place to house all keepsakes you've collected yet prefer not to store (nor display) inside your home. Don't take the bait and get reeled into reliving the "good ole' days" by reviewing all the items. Your time is far too valuable. At this point, we are just in the scavenger hunt and gather phase. Once you're organized, you can embrace all that is "warm and fuzzy" at a later time.

Common minor zones include:

- Elementary, high school, college keepsakes (old ID Cards, report cards, yearbook, etc.)

- ❋ Handwritten cards (sorted into the nearest holiday)
- ❋ Movies and films (VCR tapes, reels, slides, etc.)
- ❋ Pictures (loose photos and photo albums)
- ❋ Extended family keepsakes (items from parents, grandparents, loved ones)

Sports / Kids / Pet Gear

Think of this Zone like the aisles in a sporting goods store. Visually, this will help you organize the Minor Zones accordingly.

Common minor zones include:

- ❋ Camping/Hiking: backpacks, tents, sleeping bags, air/foam mattresses, cooking gear, propane stoves, lanterns, and spare clothes.
- ❋ Child-related gear: car seats, strollers, playpens, rocket launchers, bubbles, sidewalk chalk, etc.
- ❋ Fishing/Hunting: camo gear, guns and ammunition, decoys, target practice items, etc.
- ❋ Park Play/Tailgating: tent, chairs, tables, umbrellas, pull wagons, coolers, sports bottles, frisbees and kites, etc.
- ❋ Pet gear: cages, leashes, toys, back stock of food, and personal care products.
- ❋ Sports: football, soccer, baseball, basketball, dance, lacrosse, etc.

Travel

This Zone represents items needed while away, and the gear required to make it happen.

Common minor zones include:

* Suitcases, backpacks, duffle bags, packing cubes etc.
* Comfort gear: travel pillows, ear buds, etc.

Work / Charity / Faith / School

Think of this Zone in terms of purpose. Do you really, really, really need to be the sole keeper of all these items? Could some items be returned or passed along to the appropriate affiliation and stored at its commercial office instead? Not sure? Take a few quick pictures of things and text to people who can help you decide and who can also facilitate the pick-up and drop-off of such items.

For the items you absolutely, positively must store in your personal residence, determine whether it should be stored in the garage or if it is better stored inside your home (if space allows). You may use some items more often if they were organized, cleaned up, and brought into your tidy home environment and not left lonely in your neglected garage.

Common minor zones include:

* Charity, faith, or school related: tables, chairs, posters, marketing, auction items, table décor, supplies for activities, and seasonal items.

* Work related: posters, marketing, A-frames, and back stock supplies

ATTACK PHASE

Purge and Process

Garage attacks are all about pacing yourself and not burning out the excitement too early or too quickly! It's time to purge and process.

Assemble your boxes and line up your totes. Use your Sharpie marker to jot down potential Minor Zones on painter's tape or bright paper to adhere to the boxes. I prefer not to write directly on the box fronts this early in the organizing phase. It's highly likely your titles will change, and you'll have ruined the front surface of a fresh, clean box. When you find small, similar loose items (e.g., nails/screws), then just gather up and place in a baggie and chuck that into the tools box in the Household Zone. This phase is all about getting your mojo moving while gaining more confidence in your decision-making skills. **Remember: *The more decisions you make, the less energy it will take.***

The Maybe Pile (yes, there's always a maybe pile!). You own a really good-quality vacuum, but the charging cord is missing. If the cord is found during your purging process, then you can store the vacuum in its appropriate zone with the newly found cord. If the cord is never found or it is found and broken, you can check the cost of ordering a new cord. If that cost is prohibitive, then let it go. If not, go online right then with model and serial number and get the new cord ordered.

Your entire garage space cannot be made up of a maybe pile, however. If at the very end of the attack phase you are still staring at an enormous "Maybe Pile" then I highly encourage you to reach out to us so we can guide you to confidently move forward instead of wandering in conflicting circles about what to keep and what to let go.

Also, you may consider having a garage sale to earn some money for items you no longer want or need but are in good condition. If you're thinking about selling items via a garage sale, Craigslist posting or selling app, go to **WurthOrganizing.com** and check out our **Garage Sale and Private Posting Printable**. It will guide you toward which outlets are best options for which items in a snap!

ASSIGN PHASE

By now, you have sorted through all your Mega and Minor Zones. Hope you have done some crazy cartwheels to celebrate this killer accomplishment! Now is the time to assign the final system for the space to house only the items you are keeping.

Shelving

Bare-Bones Budget: A no-tools-required 5-Tier Shelving System made by Blue Hawk® available through Lowes has always been one of my go-to budget favorites, and the cost is under $50. The posts snap into the bases for each stacked section. The unit typically comes in platinum or black and can hold two banker boxes or two totes per shelf section.

Moderate Budget: The InterMetro® Shelving System is a stellar solution offered nationwide through The Container Store. It is a create-your-own-rack system. Select the width and depth of your ventilated shelves or basket shelves. You can let it stand stationary or pop on wheels for further mobility. It works for everything from laundry cart drying units to housing sport balls. It is offered in white, chrome, black, or platinum finish.

Another moderate option is the Elfa Shelving System also offered nationwide through The Container Store. It is a fantastic value for the money. The entire metal system is suspended from a hearty top utility track where hanging standards slide in, offering both horizontal and vertical support. Snap in ventilated or solid shelving, drawer runners of different depths, and a variety of utility board and hook options. Think of Elfa like Lego shelving systems that offer unlimited vertical and horizontal possibilities. It is offered in white or platinum finish.

Fancy-Pants Budget: Built-in cabinets offered through your local garage cabinet supplier will give your garage space a totally finished look. Remember, you still need to corral each Major and Minor Zone on each shelf via a pullout basket or tote system. If you don't, you become what I call a stuffer; things look good from the outside, but don't open a door or the avalanche of your corralled clutter will take you down my brothers and sisters!

Really fine-tune each Minor Zone and select a cabinet product that not only is wide enough per tower, but deep enough as well. In order to truly make this investment work for you, choose adjustable shelves (rather than fixed) so you can adjust your space as your inventory changes.

Color Schemes

Pick a color scheme. For the garage? Absolutely! It is one of the biggest spaces in your home!

Consistency in your color scheme, whether it is accent paint on the back wall or storage tubs on shelves, brings that finishing touch to your garage. What vibe do want to feel when you arrive home? What color schemes speak to you and your home style? I hope the suggestions below get you motivated enough to finalize what scheme defines your space.

I recommend selecting one foundational color and then one or two accent colors. For example: grey and white with accents of red, yellow, aqua, or black. Maybe there is a school or sports team logo or flag you would like to hang up so your color scheme selection can simply follow suit.

Make your metals match. For metal shelving, be mindful of keeping it all the same finish whether black, chrome, or platinum. A simple spray paint can quickly do the trick to tie it all together nicely. The same holds true with your colored tubs. This is one of the most important steps in making a visual impact that is also cohesive in design. You want your finished design to say "WOW" and not "What is going on in here?"

For odd shape/colored items, such as my Christmas tree, fold over a solid piece of black fabric to "neutralize" the color scheme item. An oversized plastic table cloth or spare sheet is also an option that works well. It is better to cover these items in a way that is visually discreet (black), rather than storing it in a jarring red tree bag that could make the space look disorganized and disjointed.

Storage Tote Selection

Colored vs. Clear Totes. Honestly, ask yourself if you really need to see these items every single day of your life? Do you really want to display all your personal belongings to others working at your home or to neighbors who might be tempted to make them their own? Colored totes are hands down my top suggested choice in garages for a gazillion and one reasons. However, it is your garage space and not mine so lean toward what suits you and your needs best!

If choosing clear storage, glue dot the corners of a clear protective sleeve and adhere to the inside front of your clear bin. Then slide in a solid piece of white matte paper or letterhead with a nice framed border and label the box. At least the content of each bin is not blatantly visual. For clear bins that contain items you desire to keep but rarely use, we recommend wrapping the outside row of bins in a fabric remnant or cloth to neutralize its visual prominence as you enter your garage space each day. You won't realize the amazing difference until you see your before and after pictures.

Snap-on Lid vs. Hinged. Regardless of the totes' color, we recommend a snap-on lid style rather than a foldable top lid for all residential purposes. Stay away from any totes that display white vertical streaking on the base and corners for it shows the product's weakness in construction. Here are some other reasons we prefer the snap-on lids:

* **Overall more durable construction.** Once the folding hinge snaps off, you're left with a lidless tote. Topless is not a good organizing look.

- **Each tote can carry and store more weight.** Hinged lid totes can't carry the weight when sitting on top of one another; therefore, breakage occurs more often.

- **Space saving and safest option for stacking.** To keep kids and furry friends safe, stack about 3–4 maximum.

- **Easier organizing access.** It is far easier to pop a lost item into a lidded tote than dismantling a tower of hinged ones to gain access to one below.

Hinged and clear totes are best for commercial use, such as the craft supply room at our church. All our lightweight crafting supplies are stored in hinged lidded totes on shelves labeled with a number 1–50 that corresponds to the contents stored inside (tapes, glues, pipe cleaners). There is a master resource binder book attached to a workstation, which serves as an easy reference for the hundreds of volunteers of all ages who are looking for certain supplies. In addition, it prevents totes from being topless, especially in a professional environment! My goodness, where are our manners?!?

Once you've set a color scheme and are ready to purchase your storage totes, here are great options for every price point.

Bare-Bones Budget: We suggest dark-colored banker boxes with lids. Generally, this is a short-term solution since moisture and bugs could damage the contents of your box. Before filling the box, it is best to line it first with a small office garbage bag, fold over the bag over the box edges like you would fold a trash bag over its can. This protects the items inside from moisture and makes transferring to another container much easier if needed. Once the box is filled, cut or lay the excess bag on top of your sorted items so doesn't look tacky and distracting once the lids are placed on.

Milk crates are another inexpensive storage option. Oftentimes, you can pick them up for free from your local grocery store or find inexpensive options online in endless colors. Select a style with the tightest weave pattern or place a solid piece of cardboard on the bottom to prevent items from poking through the.

Moderate Budget: For those that must have clear totes, I suggest Sterilite® with snap-on white lids. These are offered in so many sizes that they are a great value for the money. It is best to keep the tote lids in the same color since different colored lids may disrupt your color scheme. A quick swipe of a Magic Eraser keeps the white lids from looking grubby over time.

A similar option is Sterilite colored totes with snap-on lids. The 18-gallon size is a great value and the inside offers the most storage capability I've seen on the market. The totes usually come in white, grey, black, and shades of blue.

Fancy-Pants Budget: For those who prefer clear, I recommend Sterilite Weathertight totes. They are great for storage needs around the home as well as for camping or boating. The super-strong latches secure the lid to the base, providing an airtight and weathertight seal. They also have handled sides with a reinforced bottom for added strength for stacking.

For those that prefer color, the Sterilite Black Stacker tote series with locking latches is a solid product. The tote is offered in a number of shapes and sizes that can be integrated and stacked together to conserve space. Another stellar and reliable option is the Commander Tote®–a black tote with a snap-on yellow lid. They're extremely rugged and ideal for use in storing heavy or highly valuable contents in a garage or shed. The matte finish disguises scuffs, scrapes, and dust. They are incredibly solid all around and I have yet to see the snap-lock yellow lid ever split or warp over time.

Wall Rail Systems

Decide what is important enough and used frequently enough to be safely hung on a wall rail system:

Let's start with long-handled items. Select your top weekly go-to items (brooms, mops, vacuum, etc.) to be placed on a rail system and then store the less frequently used items (light bulbs, extension rods, extra wood trim or panel pieces, etc.). Corral the less frequently used tall items in an old bucket or old tall trash can. Place the containers in the odd corners of your garage where the garage door opens/closes. Debris likes to gather there, so the containers make it easy for cleanup and helps discourage critters from making nests. Slide a bungee cord around or through awkward items, like extension cords or sets of sport cones, for easy hang up.

Choosing your system:

Bare-Bones Budget: Select and drill thick-styled hooks with rubber or foam finishes directly into the wall. You will probably need a hammer drill to properly place the hooks into concrete walls.

Moderate Budget: Elfa Utility Rack Systems are a great solution. In this system, a single track is attached to the wall.

Hooks then snap into the track and can be added, deleted, moved, or changed according to ongoing storage needs.

To purchase the proper setup for your needs, lean all your potential items for hanging against the wall. Place all sharp-edged items (like shovels) upward to avoid injuries and less sharp items (like brooms) facing downward to maximize space. Once all items are leaning upright, take a picture. Make sure you measure for the right length utility track and determine the variety of hooks needed to accommodate as much as possible. The track comes in platinum finish and accessory hooks come in platinum with black-foam finished edges to avoid future damage on your equipment or yourself.

Fancy-Pants Budget: The Gladiator GearTrack® is second to none in durability and hanging strength. It can hold anything from a golf bag to a fridge, if you so desire. More robust and athletic looking in design, the system has an incredible variety of foam-covered hooks and hanging basket accessories. I have both the Elfa and Gladiator track options in my garage and truly love them both because they accommodate all our storing needs.

Utility Board Solutions

Bare-Bones Budget: Pegboards are a super cheap, classic solution and can be cut and customized in shapes/styles to meet all your workstation and hanging small tool needs. You can even spray paint the surface to go with your color scheme. Once you decide the final arrangement of where tools and tapes will be placed on the board, outline the tool with a lead pencil or label above the hook for easy reference when placing it back in its correct position.

Moderate Budget: The Elfa Utility Board system comes in platinum and white finishes and offers an endless array of snap-on hooks, trays, and holders.

Fancy-Pants Budget: The patented Gladiator GearWall® Panels range from 12 inches to 8 feet in length, allowing you to hang heavier items on the wall with confidence. Made of a high-quality composite material, the panels withstand tough garage environments, standing up to the heat, cold, and humidity of the garage. The system offers a variety of options from hanging tools to shelving for all sizes and types of sporting gear. They are a fantastic value for the money, particularly if you have large inventory to store that requires easy access on a weekly basis. Gladiator confidently states, "If your walls can take it, these panels will hold it."

Sports and Hobby Gear

Now that you have sorted all your sporting or hobby gear into respective Minor Zones, you are ready to assign a final system which may combine some of the above organizing solutions.

With that being said, I will focus on storing sport balls (or other smaller like-sized items) which is the number one challenge our clients struggle with.

Bare-Bones Budget: Any of the above-mentioned totes will work as long as they are clearly labeled on the front and have lids.

Moderate Budget: The Iris® Store-It-All trunk with wheels is a large-capacity trunk with a voluminous 42 gallons of storage space. Sturdy in construction, it features a heavily reinforced lid and bottom. It will accommodate up to a 180-pound load on its two rear wheels. The trunk itself is surprisingly lightweight when empty. The fully removable lid is secured with two lockable handles.

Fancy-Pants Budget: The InterMetro Shelving System mentioned earlier is a stellar solution offered nationwide through The Container Store. It is a create-your-own-rack or basket-style system, putting open-ventilated shelving up top for the larger, less frequently used items. Add undershelf sliding drawers to help you sort small items such as air pumps, gloves, or sidewalk chalk. The InterMetro system is constructed of commercial-quality steel with an epoxy-coated finish that stands up to serious storage needs. It's so functional that you may want several units.

ACCOUNTABLE PHASE

You have already completed the most painful part of this chapter so now we just move into what we call "Maintenance Mode = The Sweet Spot." Only you (not me) can prevent this sweet spot from turning sour. Here are a few areas to be mindful of on a daily basis as you move forward:

Eliminate All Loose Ends

A typical task to be mindful of daily, but unfortunately pile-ups happen. We can become quickly shocked from the vast volume of trash and shipping boxes spread all over the garage floor.

Action Step: Make sure you have good-sized trash and recycling bins. If not, contact your local city service provider to have additional or larger bins delivered. Based on your outside storage area, place cans in close proximity to the kitchen and garage, if possible. For stinky or messy foods like tuna or watermelon, first double bag in a small plastic grocery sack then immediately place in outside receptacles versus keeping inside where fruit flies like to nest.

Streamline Recycling

Streamlining recycling habits makes it more likely that you'll recycle. I wanted to eliminate my multiple trips returning plastic grocery bags to the store for recycling. Instead, I devised a solution that I wish I had started years ago.

Action Step: Place a spare kitchen trash can in your garage to hold any type of grocery store or Ziploc plastic bag. The top of the can is labeled so all family members can assist. Once the entire can is filled, I do only one mega drop every 8 weeks to recycle instead of having to remember each week.

Sweep the Floor Each Week

Just like making your bed, this is sooooo not a big deal people, so don't attempt to turn it into one. Dirt, leaves, grass, snow, mud, screws, rocks and food crumbs can gather daily on a garage floor, and therefore, must be removed.

Action Step: Store your dustpan/broom set close by or purchase a new one to have handy at all times. When the floor is not being used for storage, sweeping takes a whooping 4 minutes and looks sooo pristine when clean. My boys and I love using the Black & Decker® brand handheld vacuum to get in all the corners and floor joints. The power is insane and actually makes floor cleaning a heck of a lot more fun when using it.

More Repeat = Less Defeat.

Let me repeat that again...the more repeat = less defeat. Okay, I just came up with that catchy phrase soooo for sure need to start my own bumper sticker product line...or not?!?

Here's to opening your garage door with pride and not shame!

This chapter had the most themes to discuss and review (for both you and me!). The bragging rights gained in your hood will be well worth it, my friend.

 You have earned another bundle of kindling to keep your organizing flame burning within if you successfully completed the following:

Assess Phase

❑ You have studied the space and envision all the future potential

Attack Phase

❑ All your Mega Zones are clearly defined to certain areas of the entire space.
❑ All the Minor Zones are clearly marked and separated.
❑ A final purge and process of all inventory is completed per Zone.
❑ All Zones are clearly labeled for all family members to reference.

Assign Phase

- ❑ All inventory is completely accounted for, transferred into its final solution and assigned a place, whether in a drawer, rack, track, or tote.
- ❑ The entire family has been given "the grand tour" of the newly organized space and knows where all items are located.
- ❑ The entire floor has been properly swept and mopped to avoid bringing stubborn filth into your home and to discourage friendly critters from making your garage space their new home.

Accountable Phase

- ❑ You have stayed accountable by eliminating all loose ends—quickly disposing of trash, recycling, and shipping boxes each week. Additional receptacles have been acquired if needed.
- ❑ You have reduced energy output when recycling buy identifying a plastic bag recycling system that not only saves energy in errand running but is environmentally friendly.
- ❑ You have committed to your new habit of sweeping the floor each week since your dustpan/broom set and/or handheld vacuum is conveniently stored nearby.

I can see it now ... Your smile is a wayyyy wider now since organizing habits have had *more repeat and less defeat.* And man, it feels (and looks) so – stinkin' good! You are beyond ready to tackle the Office Space and take down the Paperwork Virus.

9

KILLING THE PAPERWORK VIRUS

The Paperwork Virus™ is my trademarked phrase for any kind of paperwork or paper habit that radically infects our lives or homes. It is sneaky, sloth-like, and even satanic at times, trying to lure you in. From receipt keeping to bill paying, from coupon mailers to school class schedules—the struggle is real, painful to view, all-consuming, and unfortunately, highly repeatable. We must be aware of this virus strain and radically immunize ourselves from its highly contagious impact on our spaces.

Keeping an office space organized is a never-ending challenge for me as I juggle my roles as business owner, wife, and soccer mom. Office and family life all are under one roof.

My Paperwork Salad Story

I got into the do-it-later habit when I temporarily moved my work files from my car to the kitchen island corner where food prep is handled instead of placing them directly on the desk in my office. I eventually would move them—sometimes immediately post dinner, but sometimes not until the following morning. This do-it-later habit of mine led to many heated conversations between Phil and me, until the day he reached his limit. When it came time to make a salad for dinner, he literally plopped the head of moist lettuce atop my stack of daily working papers and began chopping the lettuce into tiny squares on top of my mobile office. I was totally shocked. This is how it went down that day.

Me: "What the heck, honey? Have your totally lost your mind?"

Phil: "What? I am making dinner on our kitchen island. This space is designed for cutting food, not for your work papers. I am using the counter for what it is designed for. You are using it like an office. It is not an office; it is a kitchen island, and I need to make dinner."

He was dead right, and I was wrong. My paper habit was literally chopped and stopped. I now carry my work papers straight from my car directly to my office desk where they truly belong. I also am reminded of the chopping incident every time we make a salad. It sure does make us smile—good times, good times.

Predictable and Repeatable Facts We <u>Can't</u> Change: Just like the sun is expected to rise each day, so will the mail carrier deposit your mail. Also, Amazon will deliver your packages, emails will arrive to your inbox, and notifications will pop up on your phone. It's unavoidable.

Predictable and Repeatable Facts We <u>Can</u> Change: Because you are a newly skilled Master Gatekeeper and Decision-Maker, you may have already reduced the typical "piles of purpose." These are the piles that are predictably placed by most breathing humans on spaces like the car seat, the kitchen counter, the dining table, the laundry room, or the home office.

Why do you think this is happening? Even better, what can you do to begin breaking this biting-nails type of bad habit? You know it's not good for you, nor is it a healthy habit to tell (or sell) yourself that you'll deal with those piles "later." Unfortunately, you can't stop, until one day you get chopped like I did. Which brings me to:

ASSESS AND ATTACK — COMBO PHASE

Paperwork is such a tricky virus because it not only takes over your physical space, but it infects your mental space with equal ferocity. At times, it needs to be slain in a simultaneous fashion.

Assess your paperwork and your office function. You don't want to look at an ugly virus in this space every day. Time to rid yourself of its contagious ways and start moving towards healthy habits. I have found that having a handy guide to follow can reduce any overwhelming confusion. My process offers hope and encouragement for the future framework of what your office can and will become.

Refer to the **Office Organizing Checklist Printables.** One printable is for *home office* use, and the other is for a *business office*. Once you choose the proper list for your space, you can begin to read and work through this chapter. The following guide will begin your process of moving forward by walking you through all the steps to resolve in each area of your office space. There may be some new issues that pop up during the Attack Phase, so jot those down as needed.

Write down your office themes to prep for the sorting process.

1. Grab a stack of the brightly colored paper and a Sharpie from your Organizer Tool Kit. Colored paper is cheerful and eye catching, which helps differentiate it from all the white paperwork (mail, flyers, or other existing papers) on your desk as well as from other nooks and crannies in your space.

2. Refer to your Office Organizing Checklist to kick-start the process by writing the top common paperwork types down—one on each colored sheet of paper. Examples: Incoming mail, waiting to file, things to shred, etc.

3. These paper-related themes eventually will transition into a final organizing system during the Assign Phase when we assign items to labeled hanging file folders, wall pockets, magazine totes, and items to scan for future record keeping.

During this process, keep the floor as clear as possible so you can work safely and efficiently. If random papers are spread on the floor with no theme, then assemble a new banker box and temporarily mark it "Random Papers to Review."

Before beginning, assemble your banker boxes so you're ready to corral the paper virus. If you're wondering why you need to use banker boxes, read on.

Why do I need to take the time to assemble banker boxes?

1. You will be able to avoid another attack from the dust bunny brigade by lifting and cleaning around banker boxes instead of stacks of papers that are difficult to shift.

2. A stack of papers is likely to fall over, while papers in a banker box are neatly contained. Fallen stacks become mixed amongst themselves, gifting yourself more work. Congratulations.

3. When everything is protected in a designated banker box, loved ones feel more confident and less concerned about you "touching their stuff." Kindly assure them you will only focus on your area and your belongings—not theirs. Your progress will likely inspire them to start on their boxes next.

4. It gives you the "thumbs up" to now make significant progress and proceed, with respectful caution, if the space is shared.

5. For any shared office inventory, such as office supplies and tech gear, affirm permission to corral all shared themes, and then you can fine-tune by sorting them together later.

As you work through this phase, it is important not to point any fingers or play the blame game. You have made the smart decision to read this book. That is all the matters right now. Keep your emotions at bay by exercising appropriate emotional self-control as you try to silently work through the space. Remember not to get too focused on cleaning. It will be a hundred times easier to do a deeper clean once the current virus is contained and removed.

Once the boxes are assembled and you're ready to get started, follow the steps below:

- ✳ Temporarily mark your banker boxes with these common office themes:
  - ✳ Random Papers to Review
  - ✳ Office Supplies
  - ✳ Books
  - ✳ Things to Read
  - ✳ Tech Gear
  - ✳ Belongs Elsewhere
  - ✳ Memory Keeping (boxes labeled for each family member)
  - ✳ Donations and Consignment
- ✳ Grab a trash can, and you're ready to roll.
- ✳ Love music? Turn on the tunes to keep the momentum vibe pumping.
- ✳ Set a timer, make it fun, and avoid having a cranky attitude. Nobody likes working with a person who brings the mood down, especially yourself, right?
- ✳ Every minute matters. Chip away at it in 15- or 30-minute segments.
- ✳ Set the appropriate expectation. The virus didn't spread in an hour, so it won't be resolved in an hour.

- ❋ Negotiate for motivating prize money. I know Phil will take the kids to the park for me in exchange for a serious foot rub if I complete a project important to him.

- ❋ Congrats on corralling everything on the floor into your sorting review boxes!

Clear the Desk Surface

I recently did a Skype session with a client who hadn't seen the top of her desk in seven years. It wasn't because she didn't try repeatedly, but rather, it was due to the 100+ tiny decisions that needed to be made. It's as though her desk (and mind) were stuck in a fixed position from years ago—like concrete that wouldn't budge.

These are some of the most common things found on a desk surface. They are listed in order, ranging from easy-to-clear to annoying, and I explain how to handle them quickly—bada bing, bada boom. As things get sorted and the volume is reduced to its core content—the stuff being kept—it is best to consolidate and attach many of the following items to a clipboard or place them inside sleeves in a temporary binder book, so they are readily accessible.

Sorting the Papers

Business Cards

Once you have become a serious Master Gatekeeper, then ideally, you will enter any new card information immediately into your phone—before the end of the day. I like doing it while sitting in the car before I drive to my next destination. Handling future tasks with that contact is much easier from that point forward.

* **For cards where an <u>immediate</u> task is required,** such as making a call, sending an email, etc.: Staple to an 8x11inch piece of paper and place in your *pronto* pile. If you just need to pass a card's info onto a friend, then snap a picture, text it over, and recycle the card.

* **For cards where a <u>future</u> task is required,** such as manually entering it into your phone or using a handy app: Round up all the cards, rubber band them together and mark "future cards to enter."

* **Passwords:** Quickly rewrite or tape all your password paper snippets onto an 8x11 inch paper and then slide the page into a protective sleeve for easy reference. When time permits you can convert them into an existing passwords book or purchase a new one. If you prefer something more mobile-friendly, then investigate some clever password apps to download. I prefer having two password books: one for business and one for family. Regardless, select **only one** master password system rather than having multiple systems.

Random Notes and Info

Snippets of random torn papers and notes (about movies you want to rent, websites you want to check out, books you want to read, or inspiring quotes to post) should be handled just like passwords. When time permits, you can convert them into a final system for future reference, perhaps using the notes app on your phone. You can store them grouped together by interest themes.

Appointment Reminders

Appointment reminder cards for medical appointments and other activities should be gathered up and clipped together using a binder clip or rubber band. We will define and transfer them into a final, future reference system in the Assign Phase. This may mean they'll be documented on a wall calendar, in your phone, or in a future Brain Book.

Special Occasion Information

Birthday cards to mail, anniversaries to remember, vacation plans to research further—all items of this theme should be gathered into one area. Just like appointment reminders, these will be addressed in the next organizing phase.

Wrangle Up the Receipts

Clip all receipts together with a binder clip or place them into a business-sized envelope. Later, you can separate them into those that should be kept (for tax purposes or proof of purchase) and those that can be tossed.

Now that you have used your **Office Organizing Checklist** to write on the colored papers, you are ready for the next thrilling part (don't laugh too hard) of sorting papers into their respective categories. Just crank this phase out until you cross that finish line where all desktop paperwork has been sorted and accounted for. The quicker it is handled, the less likely you will lose money on late fees, missed payments, lost checkbooks, or unused gift cards. The money wasted is staggering. Make it your motivating factor to renew your sanity and fatten your wallet.

* **Kids' school art and photo-related keepsakes** – I will address how to go about processing all types of items—both small and large, 3D and digital format—when we talk about hobbies in chapter 11. For things specifically related to your kids, you can refer to the *Ignite the Organizer in Your Child* book. In the meantime, just gather each theme into its banker box. If you feel compelled to do a quick, rough purge, then do so. Just be mindful of the clock and try not venture down a distracted rabbit hole. We will address this subject more fully in the next chapter.

Reading Books, Reference, and Magazines Don't confuse your home office with your local public library. For some avid readers, a clear line must be drawn.

* **Reading books** – You can do some quick math to figure out how big your "library" should be. For example: I can devote about two hours per week to reading, which means an average book will take me about three months to read. If I multiply this by four (to get to twelve months in a year) that equals four books per year. If I elect to store 50 books in my in-home library, then I have inventory for my next 200 years of life. That is excessive inventory.

I'm not saying you have to get rid of anything you can't get to in a year. You just shouldn't let them take up valuable space in your office. I sorted my book inventory by dividing my favorite books into labeled banker's boxes by the following categories: marriage and family, personal development, biblical, and professional reference. Books that didn't fit in those categories were either added to a books to read in the future list and stored or were donated. It was good to relieve the pressure I felt from having all those books to read. I felt confident in my decisions because I knew they were well thought through. If you prefer a more digital method, you can create your list in the notes section of your phone.

* **Reference books** – Is the content truly current, or is it outdated? Is the information readily available online (eliminating the need to store a large volume at home)? Maybe it would it be better used as professional office décor, out of your work space. Or maybe it should just be donated to your local school or public library.

* **Magazines** – I suggest canceling all magazine subscriptions until you are caught up on your existing reading. It's just way too much pressure to keep up with all that reading. Quickly sort through all the volumes. Bag them up to pass along to a friend, your doctor's office, a public library, or to the recycling bin. Guilt be gone.

* **Memorable info to keep** – You read something profound in one of the above sources, but you don't want to tear out the page? Just snap a photo of the

written page, decorative image, or tasty recipe, and save the image in a properly labeled Dropbox folder or email it to yourself to save in a labeled file on your computer.

Create Your Brain Book

When you have paperwork that needs to be processed, and pronto, it's easy to feel paralyzed. How will you possibly move forward successfully from here? This is one of my favorite parts of this book because I know it will be a game changer like no other. Clients hire me for $150 an hour to teach them about the following products and concepts that you are now holding in the palm of your eager little hands.

The Brain Book organizing concept will allow you to capture the <u>mental</u> part of organizing and transition it into <u>action</u>. Witness your endless task list move from future to-do lists to actually done. A Brain Book gives our miraculous mind the freedom to focus on producing work and ideas that are creative and current rather than forcing our subconscious to continually remember actions that are required. A Brain Book can easily do the work for us. Bottom line—it's not smart to drain your brain of its powerful energy and its potential.

Divide Your Tasks by Type A gazillion years ago, I read the organizing classic *Getting Things Done* by the efficiency expert David Allen and had an epiphany. It was the miraculous understanding that there is a far better way to work and that it is essential to understand how and why poor work processes impact our brain. In the section of his book called No-More Daily To-Do Lists, Allen explains:

✳ Trying to keep a list in writing on the calendar, which must then be rewritten on another day if items don't get done, is demoralizing and a waste of time. The "Next Actions" lists I advocate will hold all of those action reminders, even the most time-sensitive ones. And they won't have to be rewritten daily.[2]

Because his book was written in the days of the Blackberry, I decided to combine Allen's "Next Actions" list concept with my phone and a personal organizer agenda book to create my Brain Book. I fully agree with Mr. Allen on the importance of tackling projects through to completion instead of wasting brain energy looking through a massive to-do list with all different types of tasks mixed together. Amen, brother.

Instead, I recommend a technique I call *flip and focus*. Organize brain book tasks into the types of things you can tackle at specific times of day, such as working on project emails at night or making calls during the day. Some common task types that can be used to label the pages are: Calls, Office, Ongoing Projects, Errands, Family, and Home.

As mentioned earlier, I don't like to mix business with pleasure, so I prefer keeping my personal list separate from my business one. Additionally, I find it helpful to temporarily hold a time slot by noting the suggested time with a mechanical pencil. When other parties reply, you can easily change the time or, once confirmed, write it in ink. Lastly, I use a highlighter to further emphasize important events.

---

[2]   Allen, David. *Getting Things Done: The Art of Stress-Free Productivity* Penguin Press, 2001.

Brain Book Options

Bare-Bones Budget: Grab a small, bound notebook—no bigger than 6 x 9 inches, so that it is travel-friendly and not too heavy to carry (either alone or when placed inside a purse or laptop bag). Grab a ribbon or twine and attach a pen to the spiral or binding seam so you are never, ever, without a pen to document all the brilliant ideas that will flood through your brain. You can either designate one page per task type, or you can divide one page into four or more sections.

Moderate Budget: After nearly a year of searching and working on designing my dream organizer in terms of style, size, and layout function, the organizing heavenly gates opened and landed my eyes on the most angelic 6 x 9-inch personal planner: Exacompta Weekly Desk Planner – Space 24°. Also, after many sad lost-pen moments, my discovery of the Pen Loop made by Leuchtturm1917° turned that frown upside down. Now, I just peel and stick the elastic loop onto the back-leather cover of the Exacompta Planner and slide in my preferred writing instrument. Can you hear the harp music playing now?

Fancy-Pants Budget: I have yet to find an organizer I like more than the Exacompta. I think its function is pretty fancy, but its price is not. It's an excellent value for the money.

Now it's time to marry your mind and your organizer. Place your right hand on your Brain Book like it was the Holy Bible and slowly repeat the following sacred organizing vow:

I, _____, Organizer Guru, take you, Brain Book, to have and to hold from this day forward, for better, for worse, for richer, for poorer, in sickness and in health, till death do us part. I do solemnly promise from this day forward to never ever, ever, ever "drain my brain" power by voluntarily documenting my daily and future tasks on endless post-it notes and random notebooks in my home, office, or car instead of using my Brain Book to support me. If I am ever without my book partner, then I vow to jot down my thoughts. When reunited, I will immediately binder clip the note to my book, and then transfer into the book at the end of the day so I don't ridiculously engage in a foolish, unproductive behavior and unhealthy organizing relationship with myself.

Master Calendar System

Eons ago, I worked with a realtor to organize her office. She had arrived late to our session because she was confused about the day and time, despite the fact that I confirmed it just a few days before. This happens often with new clients, so I didn't think more about it until we began sorting through her office and desk space. We discovered that she was maintaining five calendar systems: one on her phone, one on her desk, one on her wall, one in the kitchen, and last but not least, one in her purse.

Even she couldn't believe she had been using so many calendars. The realization helped her understand a source of her daily exhaustion. I couldn't imagine how she had been functioning— how she was keeping track of what to do and where to go each day with all these calendars floating around?

Multi-Step Projects

Multi-step projects take *more* than two minutes to complete and involve more than one step to complete. As I read further into Mr. Allen's book, he discussed how much more efficient it is to organize a multi-step project into its individual steps. I immediately corrected myself by separating the "starting task" and the "finishing task" on the weekly list in my planner.

For example, if there is a crack in your windshield and the glass needs to be replaced, instead of writing the finishing task of "replace windshield" on your list, write the starting task, which is "contact claims department about cracked windshield."

1. Grab a binder pocket folder and place all car-related info inside with a few lined pieces of paper for taking notes when working on the go.

2. Mark the full name of who you spoke to in the claims department and any related reference number from the call.

3. Contact the windshield provider to schedule your appointment and jot down the name of your appointment scheduler as well.

4. Introduce yourself to the installer, inspect the work, and speak up if you are dissatisfied so corrections can be made.

5. When the work is complete, add the receipt to your folder which is then placed in your "Waiting For" zone on your desk or in a drawer until you have been reimbursed from your insurance.

6. Once reimbursement is posted you can either staple the paperwork and file in your Car Insurance file or scan the documents and place with other monthly bills for future record keeping.

7. If a paperless method is preferred, then use the notes app in your phone for documenting and a scanning app for storing any related documents.

IGNITE THE ORGANIZER IN YOU

As our session concluded, she walked me out into the hallway where we spotted another calendar pinned on the wall, and we both burst out laughing. The discovery of this sixth calendar was another reminder of her previous challenge with time management. But that was in the past now because we had already identified and set up her new Master Calendar System. As I drove away, I grinned widely knowing her time struggle was over and easier days were ahead.

Calendar Options

One of the reasons many people have trouble selecting just one calendar system is that there are infinite options to choose from. Below are the top fan favorites (both from my personal experience and those of numerous clients).

These choices are not only the easiest to implement, but also the easiest to maintain long term:

iCloud Calendar

1. Create and manage one or more calendars using iCloud. com. Access calendars on any iOS device or computer that has the iCloud Calendar setting turned on.

2. Open your Gmail account, if don't have one, create a free one and you can use it solely for calendar purposes, or you can use it for both calendar and email.

3. Next, subscribe to the iCloud calendar from your Google calendar. In iCloud, click the share button to the right of the calendar to share any type of calendar you create. Customize each with color coding.

4. When creating a new event, select which calendar to post to. For example, my personal doctor appointment is posted on my personal calendar, which is color coded in green and only viewable by me. Client sessions and speaking events are posted on my Team Calendar in purple and only shared with my team members. Lastly, all family events such as family trips, kids' games, etc. are posted on our Family Calendar in yellow and only shared with Phil. My favorite part is that it documents who created, edited, or deleted an event (this has saved many marital arguments on who didn't notify whom about an event). The app does the documenting and reminding for us, I seriously love that feature the most.

Microsoft Outlook Calendar

This is a common application in the corporate business world, and there are a ton of YouTube videos that explain how to use this calendar to its full potential—from setting alert reminders to inviting other parties to a scheduled event. Unfortunately, the platform currently does not have the capability to integrate with either Google or iCloud calendars, so my hubby uses it exclusively for his client appointments. However, he knows he must look at his iCloud family calendar on his phone to ensure none of his late-night meetings conflict with carpooling for the kiddos.

Tech Alert

If you are not tech savvy and are seeing stars reading this section, no worries. Grab your Brain Book and jot down all your tech needs as well as any passwords and email addresses you may need for your calendar. Then, set an appointment with a family member, friend, or a hired technical service to get help setting up your calendar system.

Before you do all this, make sure you believe it is user-friendly and will meet your needs. It doesn't matter how great a system it is if you won't use it. During setup, don't be afraid to ask any tech-related questions you might have, and be sure to articulate how you currently keep track of things to help make sure the system is set up properly for you from the start.

Technology is an area I have found to always be worth an investment. When you have a good system, the time conserved is truly immeasurable. If you don't have the tech skills, I recommend hiring an expert to get you set up. Often, the errors that occur when attempting to do it yourself cost far more than any initial investment in proper tech set-up from a trusted technical guru.

Paper Calendar

In my office, I print off calendar pages for the four upcoming months and post them above our main work desk. Each month is 8x11 in size, so we can easily see upcoming events at a glance in our work-zone area. For personal appointment keeping, however, be sure to select a travel-friendly calendar size to carry with you so appointments can be confirmed wherever your day may take you. It is one less thing for you to document upon returning home.

Hybrid System—Digital and Paper

I enter all my scheduled appointments into both my paper planner and my phone. The phone reflects all my personal and team appointments, so at a glance, it gives me the "big picture" of what the upcoming week will look like. For all events where prep is required, I enter it on the iCloud calendar with two reminders—one alerts me the day before so I can prep myself by loading my car the night before to avoid racing out the door like a woman in maniac mode and the other alert notifies me one hour before the event. I then also mark the event in my Brain Book, so I can fine-tune other related tasks to prep in the days leading up to the event.

Time Management Tip

For a multi-day event, such as a family trip or hosting the holidays, I block out many days both before (for prep) and after the event (to catch up), so I don't overload myself. This allows time to organize and pack beforehand, and to do laundry and get to the grocery store afterwards. When possible, allow yourself that cushion to catch your breath before you launch into the next scheduled event.

ASSIGN PHASE
Power Through the Paper

I have a few tips for you as you start to work your way through all your paper:

First, don't mix business with pleasure. This old saying also holds true for your desk space. A few years back, I started keeping my business-related paperwork on the left side of my desk and personal paperwork on the right. I found that this division of desk zones allowed me to prioritize my work more efficiently and resulted in less confusion.

Once the work and personal separation has been established, I recommend you approach the piles for each category in the following order:

Pronto Pile – This stack requires urgent attention to complete. Crank it out first until it's completed.

Inbox Pile – This stack requires attention, but not as urgently as the Pronto Pile. Sort through and arrange with the most important tasks at the top and least important at the bottom.

Waiting For – For these papers, no further tasks are required on your end. You're just waiting for someone else to bring the project to completion (such as your insurance company reimbursing you). The papers in this pile can be filed when all the tasks are completed.

To Be Filed – No further tasks are required in this pile. These papers just need to be filed or scanned into a corresponding folder on your computer. For paper filing, my favorite option is to use hanging file folders with clear tabs that you can stagger. They last a long time and are easiest to see at a glance. Manila folders bend too easily for daily use, so save them to store documents for tax time and donate the rest.

Going Paperless

Do you want to make the jump to paperless but are not sure of the best way to go about it? I suggest transitioning one file theme at a time. Get used to the new system before you begin converting the next category.

The following steps can help get you started:

* Select a File Theme: Home, for example.
* Start with the nonnegotiable vendors first, such as mortgage payment or landlord.
* Contact the vendor on phone or online to set up autopay billing from your bank account.
* When you receive the monthly statement by email, review it quickly for any errors.
* Save the statement (like you would in a physical file folder, but now save it digitally in pdf format).
    * Example: Home File Folder - ABC Mortgage: March 2019.
* Go back to the vendor's email and archive it.

File Format Options:

When it comes to filing formats, I have two suggestions.

Option 1: Purely A-Z Format, Mixed File Theme: Meaning no matter the category, (home, or medical) all your files are kept in alphabetical order. This is an option only for those with memory's strong enough to recall all vendor names, otherwise much time can be wasted searching your entire alpha system for one file.

For example, **A**BC Mortgage, **B**e Clear Vision Plan, **C**ellular for Life, **D**one Right Home Insurance, **F**oot and Ankle Specialists.

Option 2: File Themes by Color, Then A-Z Format: Meaning you create a category based on color (e.g., red hanging folders or tabs represent your red brick home). Then within that category, all your vendor files will be placed in alpha order (**A**BC Mortgage, **D**one Right Home Insurance, etc.). Green can represent your health, and health care providers and vendors hanging files will then be placed in alpha order (**B**e Clear Vision Plan, **F**oot and Ankle Specialists, etc.).

Personally, **File Themes by Color, Then Alpha Format** is an overall fan favorite because the colorful hanging files are not only cheery to look at, but they make it easier to differentiate file themes from one another. This format also doesn't force you to recall things in pure alpha order, which can make finding an exact vendor name challenging. Instead, you go directly to a specific file theme and then narrow your options from there.

It is your brain and your file cabinet, so you decide what is the most efficient format and start filing that pile away.

Tab Making – Go all caps or go home. Anything smaller is too hard to see. Label length for clear plastic hanging file tabs usually is about 2.5 inches with the Brother Label Maker so figure out how many characters that is, print off a sample, wrap the label around the paper tab insert, and slide it into the plastic tab. This will allow for added security from the insert falling out in your file cabinet.

WARNING: Never leave your financial record keeping in the hands of your vendor. It is imperative you have your own set of financial statements because vendors usually keep records for only 1–2 years.

INVEST IN AN EXTERNAL HARD DRIVE: Set an appointment on your calendar every six months (at minimum) to back up your computer on an external hard drive. Takes maybe 15 minutes max. You will thank me a million times over if, God forbid, your computer is hacked or crashes. It is important to keep the drive protected from any moisture or movement that could permanently damage it. I keep mine in a padded mailing envelope, stored in my tech box for safekeeping.

Hybrid Method—Paper, then Paperless All our personal bills are paperless except for my business, which follows what I call my Hybrid Method. It's a combination of both systems: a paper statement for note-taking, but once reconciled, the entire month's set of financial statements are scanned and then shredded, therefore making you paperless.

The **Business Printable** I created for you to download will be a helpful guide to follow.

- ✳ I take the printed statement and double-check my receipts to see that charges are correctly posted in the statement.

- ✳ The **tax category** for that posting is marked to match the said receipt (e.g., fuel expense or marketing).

- ✳ Expenses from all remaining bank and credit card statements are reconciled and placed into a **Monthly Excel Spreadsheet** broken into income or expense categories.

- ✳ At the end of the month, all income and expense totals of each tax category are entered into QuickBooks using the Spreadsheet figures.

- ✳ Sales taxes are paid accordingly.

- ✳ The **Monthly Excel Spreadsheet** and all the supporting statements and receipts are scanned in as one set onto my computer marking the **Month and Year.**

- ✳ Each scanned page is double-checked for accuracy, and all pages are properly scanned and visible to read.

- ✳ The entire financial set is then shredded.

- ✳ WARNING: If your receipt-keeping system requires too much work, immediately implement a more efficient system to conserve your time and energy.

ACCOUNTABLE PHASE

I know my office can go from fab to drab in a matter of minutes. No matter how organized I am, I have accepted the fact that my office is a battle I will always have to fight while juggling a thriving business and family life. I am, however, confident in my systems and regularly reflect on what works and what doesn't as my needs grow or change.

It is a space that is never done. Like the kitchen dishes, it is a space that is never, ever truly done for good—rather just for the moment. The better you become at Gatekeeping, the less volume you will have to sort through during office time. The longer you use these new systems, the faster your decision-making will get and the more confident you'll become as you move from task to task.

Future Gatekeeper Reminder

Once you have granted the paperwork virus access to your home, you have given yourself more work. Once the "virus" has arrived, your choice is clear. You must read it, share it, maintain it, file it, shred it, clean it, discard it, or donate it. The initial step as a Master Gatekeeper is awareness—awareness of what you absolutely, positively must bring into the home, and what you can elect to leave outside. We have more power than we realize. It's time to enforce it.

Clouded and Need Clarity?

If my thoughts become clouded, I often will take a few minutes and cut some paper for my paper-crafting card projects. Sounds silly, but this hobby allows me to calm my mind and then clarity in my thoughts soon follows. Maybe for you it's listening to music or taking a quick walk to the kitchen to refresh your coffee and grab a snack. Study yourself and learn your healthy and unhealthy office habits. Remember that all those office items didn't creep in there in the night. Someone brought them in, so it is up to you to take control and take them outta there.

Receipts with No Purpose

Take a pass on keeping receipts that serve no recording purpose. For instance, you paid cash for a coffee and donut. Because cash pay will not be reflected on a future statement to reconcile nor is that purchase tax deductible (unless you run a business and claim it as an entertainment expense), there is no reason to keep the receipt. You drank the coffee and ate the donut. Only keep what you paid for via debit or credit card for month-end reconciling and recording. Otherwise, take pleasure in taking a pass on bringing the receipt home, and instead, toss it out with your donut napkin.

Register-side Recording

Next time a cashier hands you a receipt, step aside to let all the huffing, impatient people in line have their turn. Take 10 seconds to review for errors and sort through the coupons or promotions you were given. Immediately hand back or toss accordingly. If it's a potential business or tax-deductible expense, grab a pen, circle the date, the total, how paid, and add the respective tax category. Then tape the receipt and others in similar categories to an 8x11 paper, which makes for easy scanning at month end. Those 10 seconds at the counter will easily save you 10 hours at tax time.

On-the-Go Receipt Keeping

Use only one system consistently to avoid further clutter and confusion. It must be a system you can use on-the-go. Cumbersome and bulky doesn't work. Think simple and streamlined. If you prefer a wallet, place receipts in the *same* section *every single* time. If you prefer a pocket in your purse or satchel, make sure it has a secure snap or a zipper closure. A small mesh zipper pouch is a nice mobile alternative. Be open-minded and try a few systems until you nail down one that hits straight on.

Be a Conscious Consumer

Regardless of your system, it is imperative to carefully review all your statements. Fraud and accounting errors are easiest to fix when caught early, which is possible if you are a conscious consumer. You worked hard for your money. It's important to keep track of your transactions before your funds slips through your fingers and into the hands of another.

Record Keeping

How long should you keep records? This depends on the type. For tax information, per government guidelines:

* Personal Tax Records – Three to four years for all personal documentation and supporting tax records.

* Real Estate Records – Seven years for all contract and supporting tax records.

* Forever Documents – Birth and death certificates, Social Security cards, current and past copies of wills and trusts, divorce and custody documents, and deeds to property or vehicles you currently own should all be kept forever.

When in doubt, always seek expert advice. This can be from your accountant, tax advisor, family attorney, or any other outside counsel who can advise you best on what to keep (and for how long) because tax situations can vary greatly from one year to another as well as from one household to another.

Tax Record Keeping

At the end of each calendar year, assemble a banker box, grab bright colored paper and a Sharpie from your Organizer Tool Kit and label the sheet the same title as it's folders category. Pull all paper records from said hanging file and place it behind your colored divider. Repeat until all folders have been pulled and placed in its box marking the Tax Year.

Shred old files or light a match to the papers in your nearest fireplace. Indulge in s'mores and hot cocoa while you watch it burn. I had a client who literally had a bonfire in his fireplace during our organizing session, burning old divorce and business papers that dated back over 18 years. He not only had a blast watching it burn, but said it was very cathartic to be finally rid of the documents that emotionally weighed him down for many years.

Email Management

Going through emails can take up an enormous amount of valuable time. With online purchases, signing kids up for sports, etc., it doesn't take long for us to start getting literally hundreds of emails each day. The first step to get control of this beast is to immediately go to UnrollMe.com and download the free app. In minutes, you will be able to clean up your inbox.

This off-the-charts amazing app is a life saver. In just moments, you can select which subscriptions you want to continue being sent to your email and when you want to receive these communications—it can be at a certain time of day or a specific day of the week. In seconds, you can also unsubscribe from unwanted emails.

Each month UnrollMe.com will send a notification of how many new subscriptions they detected. For me, the number is staggering. Even though I am a solid gatekeeper and do all that I can to keep my email address confidential, there are, unfortunately, companies who sell my info or add me to lists without permission. I love this app because it helps me keep track of who has my email address and gives me tools to stop unwanted contact.

Organizing Emails

For emails you desire to keep, just click the Archive button and it is saved in your email system forever. If there are emails, you'll need to easily reference, you can create and label folders (with project or clients' names, for example), then drag and drop related emails into that dedicated folder in your inbox.

You can also create tabs in your inbox for all emails that are social, travel, and promotion-related so they can automatically be placed there when they arrive in your inbox. What a time saver—just love that feature.

Multiple Email Accounts

Lastly, I highly recommend that if you have more than one email account that you hire a tech guru to help you coordinate the account settings so they can both feed into one account for easy viewing. When you go to reply, you can select which account you desire to reply from. This is another mega lifesaver tip and worth hiring someone to get it done correctly the first time.

High five to you for killing the paperwork virus. I can only imagine how many stacks of papers were slain! Raise your sword in victory for a battle well fought.

You have earned another bundle of kindling to keep your organizing flame burning within if you successfully completed the following:

Assess Phase and Attack Phase

☐ All loose **business cards** are gathered, and a future reference system has been decided: originals placed in an old-style bound book, manually entered on your phone, or cards scanned via phone app.

❑ All **passwords** are gathered, and a future passwords system has been decided: passwords are either temporarily entered into a small notebook, you have purchased passwords book, or entered into an app or notes section on your phone.

❑ All **receipts** have been wrangled up, and you have decided what needs to be kept (receipts for possible store returns; receipts to reconcile and attach on a future bank or credit card statement; receipts to be kept for tax deductions), and those that can be tossed.

❑ All **loose papers** have been placed either: in one area to await sorting into themes; in their file destination after already being sorted; or scanned to their digital destination.

❑ All **reading and reference materials** have been sorted, and a system assigned regarding where and how many will be stored.

❑ A **Brain Book** concept has been decided upon—you will be using a temporary spiral notebook, an Exacompta® personal planner, or going purely digital with your phone, tablet, or computer.

❑ All the following have been gathered in one place to handle individually when ready (or marked in your Brain Book as a future task to tackle):

✓ Random notes – via binder clip

✓ Appointment cards – via rubber band

✓ Special occasions: birthdays, anniversaries, and vacations – Placed in a protective plastic box to avoid moisture or damage.

- ☐ A system has been identified for **mail processing** and **multi-step projects.**
- ☐ A **calendar process system** is identified for yourself and one communicating with all family members.
- ☐ A system has been identified for **bill paying and processing.**

Assign Phase

- ☐ A **Filing System and/or Paperless System** has been identified for future record keeping.
- ☐ You have identified a **system for scanning files,** if you wish to go digital.

Accountable Phase

- ☐ **Past tax files are purged** and/or disposed of according to advice from your legal counsel.
- ☐ An **email processing system** has been identified, and designated folders or tabs are created.
- ☐ **Email spam blockers** are in place and/or selected and an **email-management system** for unsubscribing has been set up.

The worst is now behind you! Let's now work to wrap up the final touches on your office space so you be most productive in your days ahead.

CREATING AN OFFICE OF ORDERLY WAYS

You've organized the paperwork in your office. Now, we need to focus on the rest of the space. I always loved watching the famous stylist Tim Gunn on *Project Runway* and the way he mentored his designers through their creative design phases by saying, "Make it work." Time for me to mentor you in the same "fashion."

ASSESS PHASE

Assess where all your "offices" currently reside: dining table, kitchen, secretary desk, or shared space in the guest room. Then, decide on the one, *single* location where you can consistently work *and*, ideally, store all your related supplies. Often one's "office" doesn't have a truly designated space or room. This may be why its contents have contaminated multiple spaces in your home, your car, and beyond.

* **Living Room Option** – If there is a long wall in a family room that can house a desk and upper shelving, then grab a spare folding table and try that spot out for a week or two.

* **Dining Room Option** – If you have a nice dining table that is rarely used during the year, try rotating it around to make it a desk. Use a coordinating hutch or buffet server to expand your options.

* **Hallway Closet or Niche** – Don't laugh. I have seen small spaces yield mighty returns by maximizing the wall space with a large, creatively painted pegboard system and an Elfa system over-the-door utility rack.

* **Noise-Canceling Headphones** – Last Christmas, I requested a pair of noise-canceling headphones so I could work in silence when my boys decided to have a wrestling match in their room next door. It turned out to be a fantastic investment for the whole family. Not only do I have silence when working, but my sons also like the peace when reading in the living room while other activities are happening around them.

Assess the future space and its function. Think about some of the following questions:

* How does the space feel to you? Which areas need further analyzing to address?

* How are you currently using this space? What works and what doesn't?

* What are the top 5 knots that need untangling in this space? Not enough surface space to work, piles everywhere, etc.?

* What activities would you like to do in this space? Check emails, make calls, work on personal tasks, etc.

Picture the potential. Taking a photo of this space may provide the most revealing assessment. I would bet you some serious cash that your pictures will show just how little *surface* space you have to work on and how much *vertical* shelf or *closet* space isn't being maximized to its full potential. Having a nice open area for you to comfortably spread out your work and your creative projects is well worth the effort.

Sketch it out. Measure and outline the space, making sure you mark all areas of the room and closets from ceiling to floor.

Progress over paralysis. You'll have the most amazing sense of freedom when you've gotten through the paper piles, old files, and the overload of endless information—an I-wanna-shout-from-the-tippy-tippy-mountain-top type of feeling. It's that stellar.

Check the condition of the space to determine if any repairs or structural/design changes need to be made. Place an X where you need to repair or reconsider your current setup. Go to chapter 6 for more details on what steps you can take here.

Doors:	__ Condition	__ Function
Shelves:	__ Condition	__ Function
Lighting:	__ Condition	__ Function
Style:	__ Condition	__ Function

Styles that make you smile. Some years ago, I hit a crossroads in my home office. My team and I had outgrown the space considerably. Either I needed to lease new office space or start maximizing the current area by doing a mini renovation.

My office furniture and accessories were dark and goth-like color, so I chose to follow the wooden sign in my office that states, "This is my happy place," and started using the colors and styles that truly make me smile. For less than $1,000, with my team's assistance, and eight weeks of diligent transitioning, the space was transformed from goth to gorgeous.

Desk and Chair Intervention

As mentioned, when we talked about Closets (where consistency in colors and style of hangers were flat-out nonnegotiable), the same principle applies for the furniture finishes on the desk, chairs, and accent accessories in your office. It is quite impressive seeing the visual impact that can result from using just one can of spray paint on an applicable surface. The cost savings from adapting existing furniture is this way may allow you to invest money in something like a new set of matching chairs.

Condition: Is the desktop large enough to work on and store your core daily supplies? Would it make better sense to pass your desk or chair down to another family member and upgrade yours instead?

Function: Do the drawers work? Can they be easily fixed with a screw driver and some WD-40? Do they offer enough storage for your core daily items?

Designer Eye: If your eye is drawn and spirit uplifted by certain color schemes, then by all means run toward those. That may be just the thing to get you motivated to spend more time in the office. After converting my own office space, I personally experienced how the new style lured me and other family members into working in it more often. If the space is shared, then strongly encourage your loved ones to be involved in the Assess and Attack phases. The more energy that is personally invested into its success, the more likely they will be committed to maintaining the space after the Assign Phase.

ATTACK PHASE

Warning: This is not the fun part. Thou shall not tell a lie, so let's just get it over with as quickly as possible together, okay? Seeing your office transition into a well-organized, clutter-free, dust-free, virus-free space IS the mind-blowing fun part. Time to stop talking and get going.

Clear the Floor

Paperwork

Hopefully, most of the papers were cleared off the floor when you tamed the Paperwork Virus. If you haven't tackled it all, you may want to take a break and work on sorting and organizing other supplies in the office and then can circle back to paperwork.

Core Office Supplies

Nothing aggravates me more when I am trying to work efficiently than being surrounded by tools that create more work to operate them. These include things such as blotchy pens and dull scissors. It is astonishingly predictable how many cups of pens, pencils, markers, and every imaginable office utensil are commonly placed on an already crowded desktop. Unless you are in a creative field—like graphic design or architecture—I highly doubt you need to access all these items every single working day.

Place a small sample of your core, go-to supplies in your desk's utility drawer, while maintaining ample supply in your office back stock. Donate the remaining items. During my office remodel, I decided to only store my favorite black Pentel R.S.V.P. stick ballpoint pens. This newfound motivation led me to remove and relocate any other pens either to the kitchen or to the donation box. I felt a surprising sense of freedom from this simple act. To this day, I grin widely when I see all the same, pretty pens lining their drawer tray. I followed suit with pencils and markers, purging and never looking back with regret.

Back Stock Office Supplies

This is where the balance of your office supplies belongs. Maintain only the items you madly, deeply, truly will use in your lifetime (not your grandkids' lifetime). You don't need 2,000 mismatched envelopes and 3,000 notepads. It's a basic math equation—estimate how often one is used up and then calculate how many you realistically need if you only use one every two to three years.

Decide the size, style, and use of the supplies you really need and will use regularly, then store the rest. I am proud to say that I have only two "to do list" pads—one is in my house and resides in my kitchen drawer; the other is in the pocket of my car door. I only purchase them when a replacement is required, and I look forward to selecting my next design.

Tech and Camera Gear

Keeping your tech untangled and protected needs to be a top priority. It takes time to constantly be looking for them, and it's too costly to continually replace them. Binder clips and cable ties will become your new BFFs for processing this theme.

* **Ear buds and phone cords** – Wrap them up tightly. Clip a small binder clip over just one side of the wrapped section. This will keep them untangled and ready for use.

* **Headset** – Use a 3M Command™ Hook to hang the headset so it stays clean and protected. These hooks offer many design options and are safe for most surfaces. Place the hook out of visual sight, but within arm's reach on your office wall or on the side of your desk or file cabinet.

* **Laptop cords** – These usually come with an included gear tie. But if your cord is too long and you prefer to add a second tie, Nite Ize offers a nice selection of organizing and clipping cords.

* **Handy-dandy tech gear to own** – My staff gave me a Native Union® Charging Cable Key Chain. It offers both form and function. It attaches to your keys and features

a wrapped power cord that is easy to use to charge your electronics. It also supports data transfer. This creation was made with durability and functionality in mind, using high-quality cables that are made to last. You'll never be without a charging cable again, which is why I love owning it.

* **Tech zipper pouch/clutch** – Because my work locations rotate daily between my in-home office and coworking space at DeskHub, I prefer to store all my tech gear in a small leather zippered pouch. This pouch also doubles as a stylish clutch, holding my company brochures and cards.

* **Charging cords, drones, and drives** – These high-end tech gadgets should be stored with care, since they can easily be damaged if they are not properly protected. Label and/or color-code the individual cords, accessories, and SD drives with a non-damaging vinyl marking tape

Personal Décor and Plants

Your desktop surface area is prime real estate—the Monopoly Boardwalk of your office. As such, I only have one picture frame on my desk, placed next to my fancy-schmancy acrylic and gold stapler/tape dispenser set. The rest of my décor is mounted on vertical wall space. Remove all décor from the desk, wipe it down and place the items in a banker box for the moment. Frames and random, memorable doodads, such as statues, vases, wooden signs, promo items that are big—all of these take up valuable work area. Any progress makes an impact, and we come back to these items in the Assign Phase.

ASSIGN PHASE
Desk and Chair Options

You must have a generous space where you can comfortably work and have good lighting to properly see papers and your working screens. Your seat needs to be very comfortable and adjustable for your height.

Bare-Bones Budget: A six-foot folding table. It costs around $50 and can be used for desk and storage areas. Place a dark tablecloth over it to cover your banker boxes of filed papers and office supplies. Place on the table a small, organizing desk solution to store only your top daily needs, such as pens, markers, paperclips, binder clips and rubber bands. Use a spare dining room chair as your desk chair or find one at local thrift store.

Moderate Budget: Elfa Desk System. You can select the tabletop finish and leg style (either solid legs or file drawer options). Multiple style and finish options allow you to mix and match to meet your needs. Pricing ranges from $200–300. They also have some great bungee cord chair options for a reasonable price. In recent years, Target® has really expanded their home and office collections, especially by partnering with the ever-so-talented Chip and Joanna Gaines. Their Magnolia® product line offers an array of stunning styles and is fairly priced, too!

Fancy-Pants Budget: Seek out an office commercial supplier or warehouse in your area. Since my hubby works in commercial real estate, we know that when businesses close down or move spaces, high-end commercial desk and chair systems are often given to independently owned office supply companies who have the warehouse to store and sell hundreds of gently used, high-quality commercial office system. When you consider the hours spent working in your office and productivity required, it seems like a solid investment.

Office Supplies

Only your back stock is stored in this location. Ideally, the entire inventory is in one location to avoid the over purchasing that can happen when stored in multiple places.

Bare-Bones Budget: Head over to your local Dollar Store and find low, wide bins that you can label on the front. You can use these to house all supplies divided into themes that make sense to you, from desk-related supplies to printer and tech supplies. Place all bins on the shelf in your closet or on a floating shelf made of melamine and supported by a sturdy L-bracket above your desk area.

Moderate Budget: Upgrade your dollar bins to storage boxes. Often called shirt boxes, these come finished in decorative paper, fabric, or leather. Be sure you have worked in your office a few weeks to ensure all your inventory has been fully sorted, organized, and accounted for before you invest in more upscale completion products. Upgrade your shelving to match your desk solution either through the Elfa® system, floating shelves from Ikea®, or rustic wooden panels through your local home improvement store. Select a finish and vibe that reflects your style.

Fancy-Pants Budget: It might be worth another trip to your local commercial warehouse supplier to check out what shelving units or upper storage solution options they have in stock. You can always purchase more upscale items directly from a private seller, but transportation of the units may pose a challenge and be cost prohibitive.

Plants and Décor

Bare-Bones Budget: Convert special photos and inspirational pieces into all one style of frame found at your local Dollar Store. Use Command Strips and hang up only what inspires you and makes you smile. If it brings a smile to your face, then you want to see it often. Place remaining keeper photos in a Ziploc and place with knick knacks in a memory bin or on a shelf in a closet nearby.

Moderate Budget: Head over to HomeGoods or Marshalls and select some small green succulents or decorative pieces that can add a pop of interest to tie the vibe of the space together

Fancy-Pants Budget: Paint the back wall with a neat accent color and purchase a variety of art and decorative pieces to really create a cohesive look. Be careful not to overdue the décor. The more open and clean the space feels and looks, the more creative your mind will be to make productive decisions.

ACCOUNTABLE PHASE

I know my office can go from fab to drab in a matter of minutes. No matter how organized I am, I have accepted the fact that my office is a battle I will always have to fight while juggling a thriving business and family life. I am, however, confident in my systems and regularly reflect on what works and what doesn't as my needs grow or change.

It is a space that is never done. Like the kitchen dishes, it is a space that is never, ever truly done for good—rather just for the moment. The better you become at Gatekeeping, the less volume you will collect each day. Here are a few ways to stay accountable as you keep things neat and tidy from one day to the next.

Put the Little Things Back in Place

From the desk's surface space to the floor, when you're done for the day, take a moment to put it all away.

Action Step: At the end of every day, return items to their place and clear the desktop. This includes clearing the desktop of pens, post-it pads, scissors, trash, receipts, and recent shipping boxes. It is important to start the next day with a clean slate of clarity.

Prep Items for the Following Day

Take a moment to get ready for tomorrow by quickly preparing outgoing mail or locating paperwork you need to review with a loved one after dinner that evening.

Action Step: Transfer all next-day items to a consistent location that will remind you to review those items. My dining table is the best location for family-related information, because we can discuss it together at dinner time. For event prep, I confirm meeting details the night before with my contact and load all my marketing materials into the car. I love knowing all I have to focus on the following day is getting ready and getting out the door on time!

Hooray for creating an office of orderly ways! This space is often the least favorite to tame but yields some of the greatest rewards, so I'm glad we worked through it together.

 You have earned another bundle of kindling to keep your organizing flame burning within if you successfully completed the following:

Assess Phase and Attack Phase

- ❑ All **office supplies** have been gathered and divided. This includes core supplies that are needed for daily usage; supplies that should be kept for back stock; and extra supplies that can be passed onto a school, club, etc.
- ❑ All **tech and camera gear** has been gathered, sorted, and a future label system has been decided upon (to be implemented when the time allows).
- ❑ All **personal décor and plants** have been inventoried and categorized. You've decided which shall reside on your desk, what will be hung on the wall, and what items must be relocated or donated.

Assign Phase

- ❑ A desk and chair have been either temporarily placed or a final solution planned, when budget and timing allow.

❑ All closet and/or floating shelf/storage solutions have been temporarily placed until the space has been consistently worked. When you feel the space meets your needs, a final solution has been invested in and installed.

Accountable Phase

❑ You have worked to keep orderly ways in your office by holding yourself accountable. This means putting away all the little things that like to settle on both desk and floor surfaces.

❑ You have also designated a next-day location for items that need to be reviewed with other family members or prepped for the next day's events.

Now that the office is behind you, we can now focus on an area that will not only be beneficial to your health but warm your heart strings as well … your Hobby Zones.

11

HOBBY ZONES

Carving Out a Space for Creativity (Not Claustrophobia)

Creative spaces are often overlooked in organizing books, yet these nooks of creativity can have a significant impact on our overall health and well-being. This is not just my strong opinion. Research indicates that a creative outlet helps us recharge from daily anxieties by reducing levels of the stress hormone, cortisol, and helps us return a state of calm, pure mindfulness to our busy, overstimulated brains. According to an *American Journal of Public Health Study:*

> This important perspective is echoed in the organization's 1946 preamble, wherein health is defined as a state of complete physical, mental, and social well-being rather than merely the absence of disease or infirmity.

Implied in this definition is the tie to health outcomes or changes in health as a result of an action; in the present case, the connection between artistic engagement and the psychosocial and biological manifestations of that connection. More specifically, there is evidence that engagement with artistic activities, either as an observer of the creative efforts of others or as an initiator of one's own creative efforts, can enhance one's moods, emotions, and other psychological states as well as have a salient impact on important physiological parameters.[3]

In order to maximize the enjoyment we get from our hobbies and interests, both kids and adults need spaces that make our activities easier:

* **Internal and physical order.** This is an absolute must in order to get the most out of a hobby space. I deeply believe everyone is fully capable of maintaining an orderly system no matter our season of life or any emotional/physical disabilities that may challenge us.

* **Organized systems.** It's important not to waste time hunting down favorite materials. A more organized system can be created, regardless of individual capabilities. If you can/did "miraculously" maintain order in your school/work life, then you should

---

[3]   Stuckey, Heather L., and Jeremy Nobel. "The Connection Between Art, Healing, and Public Health: A Review of Current Literature." *American Journal of Public Health.* February 2010. Accessed January 2019. ncbi. nlm.nih.gov/pmc/articles.

feel confident you can emotionally, physically, and "miraculously" maintain the same order at home.

* **A space that reflects individual personality.** It's more fun to work on hobbies and interests in a space that you find visually pleasing.

* **Well-defined zones.** Creativity thrives when individuals are surrounded by their treasures and accomplishments. And a dedicated space to house hobbies eliminates the feeling that you're living in habitual havoc.

From the Wishing Well to Well Done

A well-organized hobby zone will include structural and systematic organizing elements to increase confidence, sustain a predictable order, and be easily maintained while the users are repeatedly starting/finishing hobby projects. Reflect back on the Organizing Personality you identified most with and use these helpful tips so you can be more successful when carving out this space. The goal is to have working on your hobbies make you happy, happy, happy.

* **The Fast-Moving Train** – You may have overscheduled yourself with family commitments and have forgotten to leave room for yourself. Be mindful of this habit and begin allotting time to work on projects that will be rewarding and satisfying for you to finally complete.

* **The Overjoyed Collector** - Your sensitive spirit can rob you of both the emotional and physical space and time needed to pursue the joy of future projects. Try

narrowing your interests and take joy in passing along the excess belongings to others.

* **The Container-A-Holic** – There are containers for every hobby imaginable. Try repurposing all the misfit containers you have during the Assess and Attack Phases, and then you'll have a fine-tuned tally of inventory to choose from when you begin the Assign Phase. You'll feel confident when transitioning each inventory theme, and your containers of materials will look visually cohesive at the same time.

* **Formerly Known as Organized** – Time to accept this new season of your life and acknowledge which projects you can take on and actually complete and which ones you cannot. This knowledge will not be revealed unless you honestly give yourself grace during this life season. If you are at home more often, perhaps a dedicated niche or room could be a possibility. If you are working or traveling, then a more portable option might need to be considered.

* **Dreaming of An Organized Life** – Time to ditch those perfectionist ways and doubts in yourself and start getting addicted to getting it done in this new life season. Stop overthinking your projects and start completing them. You have learned a tremendous amount about yourself through this book. You and I are your biggest cheerleaders. It's time to stop dreaming and start living the organized life you deserve.

* **The Pinterest Perfectionist** – You've spent endless hours collecting images of the future hobby space you

envision. Time to table those ideas and redirect that energy into the Assess and Attack phases. Once those phases are 100 percent complete, you may gradually transition into the Assign Phase. If the budget isn't there to complete your entire vision for your space, then focus on what you can finish.

Use a folding table or secondhand item that is "good enough" until you have saved enough to order your hobby bench. Label drawers for your accessories. Clarity will continue to develop while you are working in your space and as it transitions. You may need to redefine your vision based on time and budget limitations.

* **The Chaotic Cluttered Combo** – Focus on taming and tackling current obstacles of your weaker organizing personality and then you can power through obstacles of the stronger organizing personality. Eventually, the weaker personality will diminish as you commit to working through this book.

* **Needs Buttoning Up** – What products are needed for a final button-up of the space to ensure consistency in completion? Maybe a fresh round of labels will do the trick? A magic eraser or paint is uber easy for minor touch-ups and to reduce dirty scuffs, giving everything a fresh facelift!

* **The Minimalist** – You have so many options at your fingertips because your inventory is lower than the other personalities. You may enjoy taking a class or two

about your area of interest before investing in the tools needed to support that hobby. For example, if you take pleasure in wildlife photography but you are not sure if it is a casual idea (rather than a strong interest), then a class will help you define your interest level.

ASSESS PHASE

Your Home Is a Home and Not a Warehouse

I love arriving home to a place where I can recharge my brain and body on a daily basis. I teach (and follow) this concept like a song on endless repeat. For me, my home is not a Paper Source, Hobby Lobby, or a Lowe's Home Improvement warehouse. My home is a home, and I must protect it like one. It is the sole place I can freely plug in my relaxation IV and let it drip!

The fourth bedroom in our home is only 12 feet by 12 feet, and it is also a shared space. It is one-part business office for me and my team, and the other part is a craft room for my hobbies and my boys' school-related projects. The fact that the room has more than one use impacted how we approached the organization. Assess your potential hobby space using the following steps.

Assess the space and its function.

How does the space feel to you? Do you feel openly creative or suffocated and claustrophobic? Are there areas in the space that need to be further analyzed?

How are you currently using the existing space? Will your space be a separate room, a shared room, a spare hall closet, a niche in the dining or living room, or a hobby bench area in your garage?

What are the top 5 knots that need untangling in this space? For example, do you need a generous desktop so that multiple people can have space work on their ongoing projects? Would the lighting need to be improved?

What activities would you like to do in this space? Scrapbook, paint, make cards like I do?

Picture the potential. As stated before, this is a crucial step. You must snap pictures of all four walls. If you meet me one day and you don't have your before shots, you may regret it (I will make you feel guilty). If you won't do it for yourself, do it for little ole me, okay?

Sketch it out. Make sure you mark all areas of the space, from ceiling to floor.

Progress over paralysis. You have done this before in other chapters, so by now you should feel far more confident in your skills as an organizer. Progress is where it's at baby!

Check the condition of the space to determine if any repairs or structural/design changes need to be made. Place an X where you need to repair or reconsider your current setup. Go to chapter 6 for more details on what steps you can take here.

Doors:	__	Condition	__	Function
Shelves:	__	Condition	__	Function
Lighting:	__	Condition	__	Function
Style:	__	Condition	__	Function

Styles that make you smile. By now, you likely have a vision of your space, including colors and styles. If not, it's fine! Think about the feeling you want this space to evoke. Sporty or modern? Classic or eclectic? Can you narrow your space/color combo down to three colors? Here is what I chose:

- ✳ Walls and Surfaces – Gray and coral
- ✳ Metal Finishes – platinum: classic, cool, and calming to the eye
- ✳ Accents – coral for cheery color, natural wood for texture, and acrylic for sophistication

Evaluate Your Hobby Habits

Weekly Use Inventory

These items are used most often and should be placed in desk drawers, in the mini craft drawer unit, and on lower closet shelves.

Monthly Use Inventory

Store items used less frequently in attractive containers. I used graphic shirt boxes (labeled on both sides) from The Container Store and placed them on Elfa shelving. Inventory themes for me include personal, business, craft, and future gift-related items.

Try Before You Buy/Move/Alter Anything

Place a folding table and chair in a potential hobby space and work on a small project. Assess the logistics, lighting, and storage options. Give it a good week or two before you finalize the location.

Identify Hobbies That Fit Your Lifestyle

There have been countless times when my family can tell that the week has just worn me down to nothin'. Phil and the boys will notice that and say "Mommy, you need a time-out. You need to craft some cards, Mom, and you will feel better." As I close the door to my office/craft room, I also close all cares behind. I can literally feel any anxieties slowly drain away. Crafting is like an IV drip to my soul. However, it did take some time for me to hone in on what hobby brought me the best drip power.

Narrow Your Interests

I am the type who wants to try it all. But, given the time constraints of life, I had to narrow my seven interests down to running, baking, sewing, crocheting, knitting, jewelry making, and scrapbooking. Whoa, that was quite the list! I quickly realized as a new mom that my window for creative outlets no longer included full days. Even several consecutive hours were rare, and sometimes, I was grateful for just 15 minutes. I had to narrow my interests. I now focus my energies on my top four favorites—running, baking, crocheting and card making.

Death of One Dream, Birth of Another

I found the title of this section to be quite profound in Josh Becker's book, *The More of Less.* As a renowned pastor turned minimalist author, Joshua shares through his research on how cathartic it can be when we narrow down our possessions, especially hobbies, to a certain amount.

Sometimes parting with our possessions means giving up an image that we have created in our mind of a person we would like to become. Sometimes minimizing possessions means a dream must die. But this is not always a bad thing. It may be difficult in the moment, but it may also be necessary. Sometimes, it takes giving up the person we wanted to be in order to fully appreciate the person we can actually become. Often these tough spots are tough, not just because they're hard to minimize in a practical sense, but also because it seems like we're giving up something important. What we are giving up may not always rise to the level of a dream, but at the very least we're facing the loss of something that seems particularly valuable or important to us.[4]

I couldn't agree more! When you let one part of a dream die, you simultaneously allow other qualities to thrive. I was fine letting the seamstress in me die because sacrificing the ability to hem clothes allowed my paper-crafting side to thrive. I now love personalizing birthday cards. I was fine letting the knitter in me die because while I liked the idea of making that darling, off-the-shoulder sweater, I like it even better that I was able to crochet a blanket for our family to snuggle in together. Lastly, while I won't ever complete a scrapbook for each of my sons' birthdays, each year I will lovingly give them one-of-a-kind birthday cards that they can cherish.

---

[4] Becker, Joshua. *The More of Less: Finding the Life You Want under Everything You Own.* WaterBrook Press, an Imprint of the Crown Publishing Group, 2016.

Identify your top three hobbies now and at least three reasons why they make the cut:

Hobby

1:_____because_____

Hobby

2:_____because_____

Hobby

3:_____because_____

I want you to install your new Hobby IV drip as soon as possible. It will be just what the doctor ordered for staying happy and healthy.

Hybrid Hobbies On-the-Go

My hobby time became more limited the more successful the business became and the more demanding my kiddos' schoolwork got. Simultaneously, my Bible study group took the challenge of reading the Bible in one year. This had been on my bucket list for quite some time, but I kept falling asleep while reading.

One of the gals in my group suggested I download the Daily Audio Bible® app. I selected the dramatic version and fell in love listening to biblical stories while I did my make-up each morning and while paper-crafting on Sunday afternoons at Starbucks. Seeing the mounds of cards and paper on my table, people would often approach me, asking what project I was working on so diligently. It gave me the opportunity to share the app I was listening to and let them select a card to give to a loved one.

I missed my goal of reading the Bible in a year (it took me three and a half years—ask Phil and he'll tell you that's because audio versions take longer than reading). But I cherished the time I spent reflecting on rich biblical teachings, while crafting my heart out for endless hours. Consider ways you can carve out your hobby when time is limited.

ATTACK PHASE

First, assemble and label a banker box for each hobby. Next, make space to separate all materials into the following piles: Keep, Trash, Donate, Consign, or Maybe Pile of Misfits.

It should be noted that the Keep pile will likely contain items from a number of different hobby themes—kid's artwork, loose photos, tools of different trades, tapes, glues, etc.

- ✳ Temporarily label each themed banker box with colored paper.
- ✳ Use blue tape to temporarily mark each shelf/drawer/cubby/shoebox/bin with each theme.
- ✳ Do a rough sort, as quickly as you can.
- ✳ Check other areas in your home where your hobby may have spread. Gather it all for the sorting party! Sort and celebrate. Repeat until complete.
- ✳ WARNING: We are not in the Assign Phase yet! Sort your socks off by rallying up all the duplicates for potential donates.

* Hear my mantra in your mind "My home is my home and not a warehouse." Say it with me, "My home is my home and not a warehouse."

Once you've finished the first sort, you may find that your Maybe Pile of Misfits is the largest pile. These items will likely fall into the following six categories and should be sorted accordingly:

1. I would love to use this item but don't have a need for it
2. I would love to keep this item but need to develop the hobby to use it
3. Items that are worth my time and money to clean/fix
4. Items for future consignment or direct sale
5. Goods that can be donated to help someone else
6. Memory pieces

I would love to use this item but don't have a need for it. You can pass it down to another family member, friend, or neighbor. Text them a picture of a group of items and get your answer quickly so you can move forward. If no one is interested, then donate it to a local charity that could make good use of the hobby items.

I would love to keep this item but need to develop the hobby to use it. These items can to be stored in your craft space **only** if you think there is a strong possibility you will use it. If not, then pass it along.

Items worth your time and money to clean/fix. Put the item aside in your clean/fix pile. If you find yourself circling back to it during the Assign Phase, then you know it's important to you. Otherwise, you have your answer—probably not worth the effort.

Items for future consignment or direct sale. Only create this pile if you think a store will accept these items and/or if it's worth your time. For me, Craigslist isn't worth zapping my energy if an item is under $100 in value. Only you can decide what you think the market will bear for selling certain items and what's worthy of your time. Maybe you'd rather invest that time on your hobbies instead?

Goods that can be donated to help someone else. This speaks for itself. Infinite hobbies offer infinite creative outlets for everyone—from little ones to gray-haired ones. You can help others engage in their hobbies when you donate unused items. At the same time, you will be creating better space to engage in your favorite hobbies.

Memory pieces. As a young child, my dad gave me this retro blue Rubbermaid container with sections to sort my Lightbrites by color. It literally "lights me up" every time I have repurposed this container over the past 40 years. *Decide if you are keeping something out of guilt or pleasure.* If there is a special piece that represents a certain moment in time, then place it in your memory bin or purpose it for daily use. For larger, awkward-sized items (or those kept out of guilt) consider taking a selfie with the item or lay a group of items together on a colorful carpet or poster board and take a photo. You can then print the image, slide it into a protective sleeve, and place it in a bin for safekeeping. You can donate the memory pieces and still preserve your memories!

ASSIGN PHASE

Now, it's time to assign and separate the tools of your trade so they are both organized and accessible. Whether you enjoy woodworking, photography, quilting, cross-stitch, or DIY home projects, every minute matters, so it's foolish to waste your time just locating tools and pieces required to complete a project.

Organize Items by Size/Color/Theme

I find that one of the best ways to make sure you've got your stuff stored in the right place is to ask yourself what the *purpose* is for each item is and what its usage *frequency* will likely be.

Below is a list of possible storage methods for an array of different hobby materials:

Cutting Tools – Scissors, wire cutters, standard, handheld hole punches, etc. should be placed with other frequently used items. Store the most used items on a utility board or pegboard for quick access and put others in a drawer.

Decorative Punches – Arranged by type and size. Make sure the punch shape is facing forward so items can be identified easily.

Fabric Pieces – Sort first by color and then sort by size. Depending on size and frequency of use, you may decide to toss these in a lidded glass jar or fold them with the finished edge facing out so they can be stored neatly on a shelf or in a drawer, preferably in a way that protects them from dust and sun damage.

Glove Sets – Binder clip each set together. Flip up the back side of the binder clip and slide onto a deep hook, hanging sets in size order, from small to large.

Glues, Tapes, and Other Adhesives – Most frequently used items can be placed on a pegboard or utility track. Items used less often should be stored in a labeled drawer or container with a lid.

Paper – Sort paper by size, color, and type. I store my 8x11 card stock sheets upright, in solid wood magazine totes from Poppin®. The paper is separated into solid and patterned. Small paper remnants are stored in a protective sleeve in the same upright tote or are lying flat in an old-style letter tray. My crafty friend Lorri, who is a seasoned demonstrator with Stampin Up, slides a sample of each craft paper into a clear file tab on a hanging folder, then "files the paper by color" in a traditional file cabinet.

Power Tools – Depending on weight, safely place on a pegboard or shelf out of harm's way. Color-code and/or label the corresponding charging/power cords for easy reference. Keep pesky cords neatly wrapped using a mini bungee cord, cable, or silicone gear ties.

Ribbons – Depending on your preference, you can sort by color or by thickness/style. For ribbon that is used often, store in a clear glass jar for easy viewing and access (I like to use an empty hurricane candle holder). For less frequently used ribbon, store on a shelf in a container with a lid, like a mason jar or decorative box.

Small Screws, Bolts, or Embellishments – Place the most frequently used items in a 24-drawer mini hardware cabinet unit. Make a label or glue a sample of the product on the inside of each drawer so you can easily return them to the right spot. For items that are used less often, place in clear, lidded containers, such as mason jars, and sort by color and style

Wood – Sort wood by length and width. And be sure to store it off the ground to avoid pesky critter invasions.

Once you've set up your beautifully organized storage spots, be sure to get in the habit of returning items back to their proper place. It will make the next hobby time that much more enjoyable if everything is where it should be, so you can just jump right in.

Hobby Organization Options

Bare-Bones Budget: Swap out as many possible/bins/baskets of one color or style from other locations to keep visual consistency within this specific zone of your space. Clean out and repurpose food jars, diaper boxes, milk crates to house a variety of smaller sized inventory as well.

Moderate Budget: Don't shy away from giving your craft space a dash of style and color whether creating it yourself or by using unique thrift store finds. Whatever the solution, it needs to offer a front handle or opening so your hand can have easy access. Play around with different textures from canvas to galvanized metal. If you desire to start new, the Like-It Modular Drawer System® offers the look of built-in drawers as well as size flexibility and stacking efficiency. Offered in translucent, white, and smoke.

Fancy-Pants Budget: Once you have worked in your hobby space for a period of time, you can explore options for a final organization system for your hobby materials. I like using the modular mesh Elfa® system and the Ikea® drawer cart options but get creative and design your own if that's your jam!

I loved spending some of my hobby time making improvements to my craft zone. Each month, I would add another label, bin, or box, adding another layer of love to my space. I did not set any deadlines, just invested my time in areas I felt needed it.

A warning about trinkets and treasures: Do not be tempted to clutter your nicely organized space by displaying items out of guilt. If you need to occasionally bring out a certain item for a loved one who searches to see if their gifted items are on display, then do that for their visit and promptly remove it once they leave. If you're concerned about an unannounced visit, you can take a picture of the item when it is on display, so you have something to show if they ask about it. It's perfectly reasonable to "rotate" things so all special gifts have their time on display. You want to choose only the most meaningful things to keep out, so you avoid cluttering the space you worked so hard to organize.

When my stepdad passed away, I was given the hand-painted mug I made him nearly 20 years ago, along with a set of his artist paint brushes. That mug and brush set sits on my crafting shelf, where it brings me enormous joy on a daily basis rather than being wrapped and forgotten in a memory bin somewhere. Carefully pick and display only the treasures that have meaning to you.

ACCOUNTABLE PHASE

Being a master of self-control is the key to success in this phase. I will always be tempted to add to my existing hobby inventory. There are just too many fun, crafty doodads out there! I want it all. But as we've learned, more doesn't always mean happier. How much you buy and keep should always be based on what you consistently need for your hobby. Otherwise, you're close to crossing the property line into the land of hoarding. Ouch! You definitely don't want to do that after spending so much energy making a great hobby space.

Be Aware of Your Weakness

I really, really love paper— ALL kinds of paper. I have loved it ever since was a little girl. My parents could have skipped paying a pricey babysitter and instead left me to wander for hours in our town's craft store. I would have been just so happy!

This is still true for me now as an adult. When I used to walk into stores like Paper Source or Hobby Lobby, it seems that almost every time $150 is magically pulled from my wallet and onto the checkout counter. Poof!

Years ago, when I was still mastering the art of self-control, if wanted to check out the goods at a nearby garage sale, I would purposely leave my wallet in the car. It gave me the opportunity to *pause* and *ponder* any potential purchase, then think through its *purpose* in my life as I walked to the car. I still try to implement that strategy today. Now, I tell my boys that we have a time limit; otherwise, the "poof factor" can occur. It's a fun and silly way to help keep the whole family accountable.

Invest in Trays

You read that right. Trays. Any kind of tray will work—serving trays, bedside trays, cookie sheets, etc. When you are done working on a project, gather all the related doodads from that project and place them on a tray. This protects items, prevents loose pieces from becoming lost or damaged, and makes for easy sorting and cleanup. They're also a good holding area if you don't want to pack everything away between your hobby times.

Schedule Your Stop Time

I can easily be sucked into the rabbit hole of my hobbies, losing all track of time. So, before I start working, I note both my start time and the time I need to be finished. Then, I subtract 30 minutes to give myself time for cleanup. I have a certain method for tidying up—I put away my cutting tools, properly store completed cards to avoid damage, and then I clean the surfaces where I was working. The last thing I want to do is go from a state of blissful, relaxed crafting to a frenzied, racing out the door madness to get to my next scheduled event. No thank you!

Here's to finally having a space where your creativity roots can grow!

You have earned another bundle of kindling to keep your organizing flame burning within if you successfully completed the following:

Assess Phase

❏ Understand the benefits that pursuing your hobbies can have on your mind, body, and overall health.

❏ Fully acknowledged any potential challenges in your Organizing Personality that you will need to overcome in order to tackle your hobby space.

❏ Identified your hobby space within your home and/ or garage.

❏ Narrowed your hobby interests to the top three.

Attack Phase

❏ Powered through all hobby-related inventory and placing them into their corresponding themed piles.

❏ Reviewed the Maybe Pile of Misfits on multiple occasions so items can eventually find a final home—either in yours or someone else's.

Assign Phase

❏ Designed systems to house your top three hobbies.

Accountable Phase

❏ You are aware of your personal weaknesses with your hobbies, recognize the self-control it takes to gather up loose ends on a tray, and are mindful of setting a stop time.

MAKING MEALS
NO BIG DEAL

The kitchen is one of the only spaces where most areas are predetermined for you. You are only given so many upper and lower cabinets and drawers, and if you're really lucky, a designated pantry space. Over the years, we've found that 100 percent of our clients complain about how small or inefficient their kitchen is. Yet 99 percent of them had kitchens that offered plenty of quality storage space. The contents and space were not being stewarded appropriately.

The goal in this space is to make meals as efficiently as possible, avoiding waste of food, energy, time, and money. In order to achieve this, we need to identify the areas of the kitchen that cause a breakdown in efficiency, leading to wasted efforts and time-consuming backtracking while preparing meals.

ASSESS AND ATTACK — COMBO PHASE

Just like in the garage, a kitchen needs to have designated zones for working and storing items. As you assess each item and its purpose in each zone, you will simultaneously decide who stays and who goes. If you can't decide quickly on the spot, then reassess the item's purpose once you feel a specific zone is completed.

Grab your **Kitchen & Pantry Printable** so we can identify the following zones in your space: *The Serving Ware Zone, The Cooking Zone, The Cutting Zone, The Cleaning Zone, The Beverage Zone,* and *The Food Pantry Zone.* Dividing the kitchen space into designated zones will give you a better, more focused idea of what you own and why you own it for each zone.

Picture the progress of each working zone. Take photos with cupboard doors open and then with the doors closed. Maybe all these zones are not clearly defined. This may be why your kitchen is not as functional as you would like it to be. I tell my clients to think of their kitchen zones like a spider web—intricate in design, so that when you pull or move one area, it affects another. If designed correctly, it will become a beautiful place for you and your family to nest.

Figure out what type of cook you are. The answer to this question will help guide some of the decisions you'll need to make about the organization of your space and your tools.

Do you love to follow detailed, multistep recipes, or would you rather heat and serve? Or, are you somewhere in between? My younger sister, for example, made cooking history in our house by solely and successfully making a complete Thanksgiving dinner at the ripe age of 13. She accomplished this by reading the largest cookbook (with the smallest print) I have ever seen.

I, on the other hand, preferred to stay in the background because that cookbook looked and translated like a medical dictionary to me. It was terrifying. I was the older sister, but she was in her zone jamming out to tunes from the big hair bands of the 80s, wearing my mom's apron, and cooking like crazy. To me, it seemed insane.

I thoroughly enjoyed wiping down the counters while she worked and looked forward to cleaning the pots and pans when she finished. It was then that I first realized "cooking ain't my jam," and that I preferred being the self-appointed organizer of the household. I liked to help make the grocery lists, tidy the kitchen after mealtime, and oversee our laundry chores.

I had a true epiphany once I became a wife, mother, and professional organizer. I am a "one-pot wonder" type of cook. I like making one simple meal and prepping a side salad. Luckily, Phil is great as the main chef, and the boys and I are happy in our roles as sous chefs. Anything more complicated— with multiple pots, pans, and ovens—and I am toast. I usually end up getting distracted and burning the meal.

Instead of fighting it, I fully embraced all the gifts God gave me and how different they were from the ones he granted to my sister. I realized I could have greater impact by teaching organizing to others who, unlike me, weren't born with a natural gift for organizing. This is precisely how I view the importance of each individual's role in running a household or a community.

Evaluate your surface space. Just like your office, you need ample surface space to work safely and effectively in your kitchen—usually a larger amount of surface space. To maximize this space, you must significantly decrease countertop décor and memorabilia. This will not only keep those things from potentially being ruined by food splatters, but it will also give you the room you need to work quickly and efficiently.

Evaluate your cabinet space. When organizing your cabinets, it's important to take inventory of what you own before deciding where it needs to go. So, grab the blue tape and Sharpie from your Organizing Tool kit, and start marking and assigning themes for each cabinet and drawer in the following order of nonnegotiable themes:

The Serving Ware Zone

Everyday plates, bowls, cups, glassware, and flatware. Place items in this zone as close as possible to the dishwasher for daily efficiency. The same applies to your everyday flatware drawer. Assess your current needs and determine whether your existing items meet those needs, or if it's best to consign/donate what you have and upgrade your everyday set. You could also opt to start using your entertainment pieces for every day. This is what I did with my everyday glasses. I consigned the ho-hum sets, and now we use the "happy-upgrade" for every day.

Serving pieces and table décor. Think about what type of entertainer you are when determining what sorts of pieces and décor you should have and where they should be located. I decided to move some entertainment pieces into my kitchen and use them for everyday purposes. I love that it not only saves space, but these items are also being used and seen more often.

I store the balance of my entertainment and table décor pieces on four shelves in my dining room buffet. From placemats and napkins to chargers, candle holders, and flower vases, I have a weakness for all types of table décor (just like paper). To keep from collecting too much, I am mindful of what I have. Take inventory. Do you have full sets of four to six serving placements or a variety of misfits? Look for chips on serving pieces that need replacing or metal pieces that need polishing (if you don't mind the maintenance). To keep freshly polished silver from oxidizing, tightly wrap odd shaped pieces in plastic wrap ... amazing results!

I love to spend time decorating our family dinner table. I switch the tablescape theme nearly every month—I even use place cards for the four of us. As a child, I loved watching my mom's face light up as she took pride in setting our family table, and I wanted that same magical feeling applied to my family's table all year round. Sometimes the boys help me coordinate themes and write out the place cards—we even make them for visiting friends. Have fun with it!

The Cooking Zone

Pots, pans, and other small appliances. Take a long, hard look at what you are really using on a consistent basis. Do you need four soup pots? When we downsized our home by half not everything would fit in the new cabinets. So, the balance of the cookware gear was placed in 18-gallon tubs in the garage.

We made this decision, in part, because we didn't have enough space. But we also did it as an experiment.

After two months, there were certain items that I never went digging for—not even once. I realized I could live without them and proceeded to do the unthinkable: donate parts of my cookware set. Gasp! Yes, I broke up matching sets. It's not like these pots had feelings for each other or like I was separating a set of twins! Doing so, opened up space foe items I used more often.

The same goes for small appliances. Do you need three different types of blenders? Is there one that is your go-to favorite? If so, you can say adios amigos to the others.

Gadgets galore gut check. This is one area that can run out of control like a flaming wildfire in the dry summer forest. Don't let never-used tools take up valuable space. There are so many gadgets that, at first, seem like they'd be fun to have. And some of them can do double duty—like an apple cutter can be used for making potato fries and chopping nuts. But if you've never used that melon baller and fondue set, it's time to let them go!

Spices and oils. Are you going back and forth between multiple cupboards or the pantry when you cook? Consider storing all spices/oils in one area—either near the Cooking Zone or the Cutting Zone.

The Cutting Zone

Does your knife set make the cut? You may not have thought about this, but a lot of efficiency is lost when you are using dull knives. I highly recommend that you either invest in sharpening your current set or replace them with a new, sharp set that suits your needs and budget. Once we started a clean-eating program, I realized the importance of investing in a fine cutting knife set (I like the Cutco brand of kitchen tools). I was so amazed by the difference it made to have quality tools. The investment was worth every last shiny penny.

Do you have an open surface space to cut and prep food? You will know immediately if your arms can't freely move when cutting food or if there isn't ample space to place food around your cutting board area. Spaces like these are essential in a kitchen that functions efficiently. One day I noticed how my wooden cutting boards were visually unattractive against my black granite countertops. I was due for new cutting boards, so I invested in Architec Original Gripper Cutting Boards in black polypropylene with their patented non-slip technology grip bottom. They are easy to clean and resistant to knife cuts which can hold bacteria (making them healthier than wood). Holy guacamole game changer! I freakin' love these boards for they not only look great but scrub clean and always look modern on the counter top.

Don't have a proper cutting zone due to design layout? If you have pared down all your inventory and your space still lacks a good working surface space option, then consider purchasing a small kitchen island on wheels. Remember to "try before you buy" by working on a small folding table or side table so you can see if this solution may work. Give it a good week or two before you make a final decision on the need to invest in a moveable island for food prep, entertainment space, and additional shelf storage.

The Cleaning Zone

Do you have enough space to the left and right of your sink area to properly clean all kitchen food and gear? What needs to be removed or changed to make that space more open? Have one tall pump on the counter with dish soap and another with hand soap to avoid unnecessary access to the cupboard. I always keep a tall plastic tumbler filled with soap and water in a front corner inside my sink. All sticky silverware is placed in there to soak so it doesn't get lost in the sink with other dishes. The dishwasher is loaded once, rather than several times throughout the day.

Dishtowel distress. Ideally, it is best to store dishtowels in a drawer near the sink. Are your towels stuffed in drawers with cooking mitts that have burn holes and last year's cranberry jelly stuck to them? Maybe it's time to clean and/or purchase a fresh set of some items. Remove holiday towels/mitts from your everyday space and place them in the corresponding holiday bin. When a holiday is approaching, temporarily place your everyday set in that holiday bin. Then, post-holiday, you can just switch it out again. Uber goober easy!

Clean out your cleaners. Say what? It seems like many people are in the habit of hoarding obscene amounts of household cleaners. Most of our clients have an obnoxious inventory. I asked my cleaning professionals, (aka, my crew of housekeepers) which cleaners they thought were essential. They told me they use a mix of water and distilled white vinegar on all counter and bath surfaces, and they recommend Murphy's Oil Soap on the floors, tile, and blinds. After I saw the results they got from using these simple products, I finished a few of the items I had in my cabinet and donated the rest.

Food storage set insanity. How many food storage sets do you own? Has matching the tops and bottoms of your food storage containers turned into a part-time job for you (one that you are not paid for ... pure madness!)? I quit my part-time storage job and selected only four food storage systems: Ball brand twist-top plastic freezer jars for snacks, Crate & Barrel small glass bowls with clear lids for chopped food, Pyrex glass bowls with lids for larger quantities, and Cambro brand commercial food-safe plastic storage containers with lids for leftovers. Why invest in Food Storage Sets and limit the number of sets to just four? Here's why:

1. Sets nest easily in your cupboards for easy access.

2. Sets can serve double duty from dinner prep to dinner table so less cleaning is required.

3. Food is more visible in glass and food-safe clear plastic containers, and they stack easily, maximizing storage space.

4. They are simple and sustainable for on-the go eating (and you use fewer plastic baggies).

5. Sets can be used as serving ware for entertaining, making and clean-up easier.

A note about vinegar ... it's a very versatile product. When my boys were preschoolers, I started mixing water and vinegar with a few drops of an antibacterial oil and lavender oil to make a safe, great-smelling cleaner. I used it on our glass dinner table and countertops, and still do to this day. I even use vinegar as my dishwasher rinse aid for crystal clear glasses, very effective and a huge cost savings over commercial products!

Let's talk trash. Are your cans located near the Prep Zone, and do you have a tall can for trash and a separate one for recycling? If not, it might be time to upgrade and get a matching set. If you do already have them, are the cans or cupboards properly labeled so you are never, ever, ever asked again where the trash and recycling are located?

Remember how I shared that labeling does the talking for you? Once, while hosting our Bible study group, the inner efficiency nerd in me tallied how many times I was asked where the trash and recycling were located. It was more than 20 times. I labeled the cans immediately after that gathering, and nobody has ever asked me again. Ever.

Back stock of bags. Place a handful of bags at the bottom of each can so replacements are handy when you take the trash out. Some people tell me they don't want to do this because they're worried the new bags will be ruined by leaking trash. That is not likely to happen. I've only seen three garbage bags rip and leak during my lifetime—and that was only because they had been improperly stuffed with sharp objects. Let go of that fear so you can begin working smarter. I guarantee you will notice the change when you can stop backtracking to the cupboard or pantry for a replacement bag.

The Beverage Zone

Do you need to move or swap this zone's location with another? If you read the Barista Station section earlier, you understand why you need to have parts and ingredients stored near one another in this zone. If you don't have enough space in the current area, consider relocating.

It's also important to get control of your inventory. Is your mug or cup collection still big enough to serve drinks to an entire a football team? We once had a husband and wife who owned a whopping 55 mugs. For reals! To determine the number to keep, I suggest following this guideline: take the number of family members in your home and multiply by three. That should give you ample inventory in this area. We own six everyday coffee mugs and eight white ones for entertaining.

The Food Pantry Zone

Wondering where all your money has gone? Check the stinkin' pantry, people! Whether your pantry is a reach-in or walk-in, all foods need to be visible to the eye and accessible to the hand. Otherwise, we lose track of what we have and may find we've wasted several hundred dollars of food.

It might be that something was opened but not properly sealed/ contained before being put back in the pantry. Or maybe, because you couldn't see it, you have jars, cans, and packages of things that are well beyond their shelf life. We once found items in a pantry that had been expired for eight years! These are facts and not dramatics.

Do you have all the same food themes gathered together or are they scattered on different shelves or drawers? Think of your pantry like your newly organized clothes closet. Just like all your go-to tops are hung in one place, place food themes you use more often at eye level, and those that are used less frequently can go up higher. Are any drawers broken or do you need more shelves? We will get into division of pantry food themes in more detail in the Attack and Assign Phases.

Fridge/Freezer Control

When you empty your dishwasher, you don't place these daily items on one shelf one day, then place them on a different shelf the next time ... right? If you do, then a serious Skype intervention may need to happen between us! With that being said, why would you approach placement of your food in the refrigerator or freezer in a haphazard fashion? Some people may need to consider zipping into a hazmat suit to empty it all. Regardless, in my mind, I feel the level of importance for this space is equal to any other in your home.

Think like a nutritionist and store everything by food group. Just like in the pantry, designate themes for each shelf and label each accordingly. For the fridge, I like beverages up top, food for making lunches in the middle, leftovers/lunchboxes on the bottom shelf, and spreads and dressings on the shelves in the door.

For the freezer, I have each shelf divided for easy meal making—proteins, carbs, veggies, and sweets. If you think this is too OCD, let me explain why I highly suggest this method. This does three things:

1. Avoids one from becoming hangry (hungry AND angry). I don't like to hunt for my food in a savage fashion. I do not apologize for wanting to open the door, find my food, and eat it as quickly as possible.

2. Avoids duplicate purchases and excessive spending. When you look on the labeled bread shelf in your freezer and see there is one loaf left, you know you

need to buy more soon but not necessarily today. This is an easy concept to implement immediately.

3. Helps all family members learn proper locations to place food when putting it away and also lets everyone know where to retrieve items when looking for something to eat. (Say it with me: let the labels do the talking for you and to you.)

ATTACK PHASE

I am going to make this phase short and sweet—like a warm, gooey cinnamon roll you just want to pop in your mouth—little decision-making and all delicious:

Use what you have, or it is clutter. You have two choices: 1) Stop "selling yourself" into keeping something that does not consistently serve a purpose in your lifestyle; or 2) Start "granting permission" to immediately implement those items into your lifestyle.

I had a dear friend who asked me to help her go through her kitchen and china cabinet after she moved. We came across a gorgeous set of tea cups, stored in their original boxes, that had been passed down to her from her deceased grandmother.

Me: These are gorgeous!

Friend: I know! I loved visiting my grandmother and seeing her collection of cups.

Me: Why are you then keeping them hidden?

Friend: To protect them.

Me: From what? You just moved, and you now have room to properly display and preserve them inside this beautiful glass hutch. Wouldn't it be nice to sit and appreciate the collection with your girls at mealtime instead of seeing a dusty set of stacked boxes? The same goes for these unused serving pieces from your wedding years ago. I would bet you big bucks that the people who used their money to give you these beautiful things would want you to take them out of the box and actually use them!

Friend: Yeah, I think you're right. I would love to use them, and I am not sure why I haven't yet.

We laughed because it seemed so logical. But for years, her default decision was to keep things boxed up, so they'd be safe. By golly, every day is a gift, so start breaking out the good stuff and forget the guilt. You either grant yourself the permission to use it, or it's clutter.

Ready to pick which sides your items will fall on?

1. Methodically go through each zone—only tackle/sort one zone at a time.

2. Gather and review all items, placing them on the counter or in a banker box.

3. Return your nonnegotiable items to their respective zones, marking the front in blue tape.

4. Jot future purchases on your **Kitchen & Pantry Printable.** Maybe it's a new glass set, frying pan, pizza cutter, etc.

5. Remaining items are either put in the Maybe Pile of Misfits, repurposed in another home/rental property, cleaned and consigned, or donated. (Cleaning hack: Use denture cleaner tablets to make glass vases or crystal glasses sparkle. Also, white vinegar and water are stellar cleaners for stubborn stains.)

6. Only put items back that you are 200% sure have a purpose in your lifestyle or household.

7. Can Memory Pieces can be repurposed for everyday or holiday use? I store my paper towel roll in my grandmother's antique wine carafe, near my kitchen sink. I love seeing it every day versus just on Christmas Day.

8. Continue the Attack Phase until all Zones have been completed.

9. Eat it or waste it. You are either going to eat the canned food on your shelves or not. There is no gray area because they will eventually expire. Therefore, be mindful and not wasteful. If you have food that is not expired, and you know you'll never use it in a future recipe, round it up and return to your friendly neighborhood grocery store to see if a store credit can be given. If not, pass it along to friend or neighbor. Who wouldn't want free food?

ASSIGN PHASE

Creating Systems for Each Zone

Labeling generously = working efficiently. Just like a decadent box of chocolates comes with a nicely labeled lid describing its flavor varieties, you can follow suit with your kitchen zones. Once you've worked successfully in your newly organized kitchen, label the side or bottom section of every drawer. For bottom cupboards, label the inside edge of the cabinet or lip of the shelves where pots/appliances are to be placed. This was the best thing I ever did in my kitchen. It has been years since our beloved ice cream scooper has been MIA = Missing in Action.

In addition, every family member, guest, or hired helper (who desires to be invited back—no pressure!) can help empty the dishwasher or set the table since all serving/cooking/baking utensils have a place to call home in your home.

The Serving Ware Zone

Nearly every drawer needs at least one utensil tray that has multiple sections or a series of same-style rubber-bottomed trays that can house your inventory, while maximizing all each drawer has to offer.

1. Take a picture and measurement sketch of each drawer. Be mindful if the drawer fully pulls out or not.

2. Based on your style and budget, either stay with misfit solutions or eventually upgrade to one cohesive solution in either in white, black, acrylic or bamboo. I do love the Bamboo Expandable Utensil Tray sold by The Container

Store. It is not only functional (using every possible inch in the drawer) but also a lovely looking natural accent for the items stored in each section.

3. If an expandable tray won't work in your space, you can always consider placing a utensil tray in the *center* of a drawer. That way you can have three sections (e.g., rubber spatulas can be stored in the left section, everyday flatware can be stored in the middle in the divided tray, and other cooking utensils can be stored in the right section.

4. Place the balance of your inventory in the Maybe Box or pass along to someone who can use them.

The Cooking Zone

Round up similar items, such as all shapes and styles of rubber spatulas, whisks, spoons, and other clever doodads. Quickly analyze and pick your top choices. *You likely only need one of most utensils* (maybe two if you have meal-prep helpers).

Keep sets of pots and pans together. Stack pots with their matching lids on, but place lids upside down, so you have the possibility of placing another on top of it.

Only use pull-out racks if you have very generous space or need them to save your back from extreme bending. The track that needs to be installed for these will reduce overall storage, and you may find that you'll need to clean out crumbs/dust in and around the tracks.

The Cutting Zone

Store trash near where cutting takes place to avoid backtracking and surface contamination. Be like the pros who always have a trash bowl within arm's reach of their cutting space. Store knives nearby in your well-labeled knife block or on a modern magnet strip on the wall.

The Cleaning Zone

All towels, rags, nontoxic cleaning sprays, and wipes need to be labeled and stored at a kid-friendly level to allow involvement from all family members. If bottles are too bulky for little helpers, then transfer solution into a smaller labeled spray bottle or have surface wipes on hand. Our rag bin is clearly labeled and conveniently placed in our laundry room along with the surface cleaner spray bottle. Any toxic chemicals should be stored out of reach of little hands.

The Beverage Zone

Adjust your shelving to accommodate your final inventory of glasses. To maximize all the vertical space in my tiny cupboard, I cut white paperboard strips to the length and width of my coffee cups, which allowed for better vertical stacking on that cupboard side. Upgrade the white board strips to acrylic once you love the layout!

Loose beverage supplies, such as coffee, teas and sweetener. For beverages you drink regularly, buying in bulk makes sense. Have a main stock near your beverage station and back stock elsewhere. For sweeteners, avoid buying in bulk because it takes up significant storage space, and you will begin noticing reduced product quality and freshness if stored too long. I am a Stevia snob, so I place extra packets in the change section of my wallet, so I am never without.

The Food Pantry Zone

There are many pantry shapes and sizes so to simplify the organization process, use the **Kitchen & Pantry Printable** to help guide you on which layout, labeled themes, and completion products best fit your lifestyle. Do not—I repeat—do not remodel your pantry until you have successfully gone through all phases. Try investing in some of the completion products suggested below first and see if they solve your issues.

Canned goods. The three-tiered Mega Expand-a-Shelf® product is great for any pantry and just about any budget. Priced at under $20, it houses extra-wide cans and condiments and makes it easy to see cans in the back rows.

Oils and vinegars. A Lazy Susan is a good option if you have enough upper cupboard space near the stove. If not, then corral these items in a sturdy, flat-bottomed, easy-to-clean basket—either near The Cutting Zone or in The Pantry Zone, depending on how frequently you use them.

Bagged chips, snack food, and cereal. Decide whether you are going to keep these items stored in the original bag and binder clipped shut or boxed in a labeled basket or transfer the contents to an airtight food container, like the OXO Good Grips POP canisters. The containers or baskets decrease ripped bags and make road trip mealtime uber easy, allowing you to just stock, pack, and go.

Tip: Organize food by meal and prep efficiency. For example, pasta boxes are put together with jarred sauces, and Asian noodles are placed near teriyaki sauce bottles. You can place like items in an open basket so it's easy to get them in and out of the pantry.

> **Identify a Budget and Meal Plan to Fit Your Lifestyle**
>
> Would you randomly book a flight without knowing the costs to and from the airport? Then, why would you randomly shop for food (that will expire, mind you) without a budget and meal plan as you travel to and from the grocery store?

Create a Family Recipe Binder

Like a tornado in Kansas, I was THAT overwhelmed by all the recipes and meal options flying around me, from written family recipes to magazine tear outs and online printouts. I needed a grounded game plan. So, with no further ado…let's create a Family Recipe Binder Book.

I have already done the hardest part and know it will be well worth the effort put forth. I have a larger binder for Cooking and a smaller one for Baking. When you are ready, on my website you can download my **Recipe Binder Book Printable**. It is an easy project you can tackle over time, so no pressure to tackle now. I go into greater detail on this topic in my *Ignite the Organizer in Your Child*, specifically the section on Family Meal Planning and Budgeting. Since Phil and I have a zero-food waste policy in our house, we started thinking and buying our food for the week like a European and not an American.

As we got older and more debt free, we found it easier to budget for quarterly bulk shopping at our local Costco because I would ration some funds each week knowing we could apply them for quarterly shopping trips there. Points to consider:

* Acknowledge that your home kitchen is not a restaurant kitchen where you must provide an elaborate menu to service multiple eating preferences.

* Decide how you will hunt for your food – Via grocery shopping or online ordering

* Everyone has a role to play – Who will shop, cook, clean up, etc.?

ACCOUNTABLE PHASE

The Accountability phase is especially important in the kitchen since this is a space in the home that is used in multiple ways and at multiple times of days by multiple family members. Being aware of and accountable for its maintenance is a must-do every day. Once you have your daily maintenance Here are a few maintenance tasks that also fall under One-Minute Rule that are essential for <u>all</u> members of your household to engage as a daily habit:

* **Wipe down the counters.** At the end of the evening. Unless you and your food enjoy cohabitating with crawling ants and annoying fruit flies, I suggest taking a disinfecting wipe to remove crumbs from the counter and sanitize the surfaces.

✳ **Promptly put all food away.** Once a meal is enjoyed, then all the components involved in food prep need to be put away. Food waste disposed in the trash, empty containers washed and recycled, leftovers prepped for a future meal and remaining items returned to the fridge/freezer.

✳ **Avoid Dishwashing Distress.** All serving and dishware must be ideally cleared, washed and properly put away at the end of each meal.

If time and energy are not available, then at the very minimum tackle 2 of the 3 tasks such as emptying the dishwasher or putting away dried items on the counter.

Once you have these habits down, you might be ready to kick things up another level. Maybe consider adding "zest" to your Spice Drawer:

Lay all your cooking and baking spices flat in a drawer (rather than standing upright in a cabinet, organized by size). I beg you to really, really ponder what I am sharing here. **Most of my clients were skeptical at first; however, not one has EVER gone back because of these five benefits:**

1. Easier for large hands to access and prevents spices from falling over.

2. Helpful for both young and old eyes—can see everything at a glance.

3. Faster access for measuring spoons.

4. Insanely efficient when the spice drawer is placed under The Cutting Zone, so you can stand and work in one place, one space.

5. Lends a finished flare to your cooking/baking experience.

Here's to a kitchen where making meals are now no big deal!

 You have earned another bundle of kindling to keep your organizing flame burning within if you successfully completed the following:

Assess Phase and Attack Phase

❑ Understood the importance that efficiency, function, and specific placement of food and food prep inventory can have on your wallets.

❑ Identified the following Zones: The Serving Ware Zone, The Cooking Zone, The Cutting Zone, The Cleaning Zone, The Beverage Zone, and The Food Pantry Zone.

❑ Truthfully embraced what kind of cook you are.

Assign Phase

❑ Successfully Assessed, Attacked, and Assigned a system for the following zones:

❑ __The Serving Ware Zone __The Cooking Ware Zone __The Cutting Zone

❑ __The Cleaning Zone __The Beverage Zone __The Food Pantry Zone

- ❑ Reviewed your Maybe Pile of Misfits on multiple occasions so it can eventually find a final location in your home or another's home.
- ❑ Finalized a Meal Plan Program with or without use of a Family Recipe Binder Book.
- ❑ Decided on a method regarding how you will "hunt and gather" for your food.

Accountable Phase

- ❑ Added "zest" to your spice collection by transitioning to a Spice Drawer.

13

LAUNDRY ROOM
LA LA LAND

Maybe you are so enthralled while doing laundry that you can't resist tapping your heels and whistling while you work, like a scene in a serene musical. If so, then please share the brand name of the laundry detergent you are sniffing, because my laundry experience is quite different.

My laundry room is not even a room; it's a pass-through from the kitchen to the garage. My attitude towards laundry is: get it done and get out of there. Unlike a feel-good musical set, my setting is more of a foul-smelling factory comprised of dirty laundry that must be processed in a conveyor belt type fashion. Let's get this space organized, so the laundry is done efficiently and quickly. By relying on some tips and tricks of the trade, laundry doesn't have to be a doomsday task. In fact, you will have more free time to pursue the hobbies we organized in chapter 11.

ASSESS PHASE

Assess the space and its function. A laundry room can turn into a mosh pit of mayhem. Laundry rooms are often used for multiple mini-tasks, such as scrubbing or soaking stains, craft projects, household repair tasks, and more. Assess whether you have enough surface space to do the tasks you need to complete. Are your laundry baskets the proper size to accommodate your weekly volume, and is there a designated place to store them? Do you have a designated area where you can line dry items that can't go in the dryer or does it obstruct your work area? Could you use a rolling or folding clothes rack in a nearby space, such as the garage? What about storage for detergents, stain removers, pet food, or other items related to the tasks assigned to the laundry room?

Picture the potential. Take photos of the room from all four sides, floor to ceiling, and with open cupboards and drawers to see potential storage options. Remember side walls and back walls behind doors which can be valuable real estate for hanging storage. Do you have multiple "make-do" solutions, such as plastic drawers, mismatched containers, or shelves? Don't worry. We are going to give you a consistent theme in the assign phase.

Sketch it out. Make sure you mark and measure all areas of all the cabinets and any potential wall space (in the open and behind doors).

Progress over paralysis. Maybe this space has been neglected for many years and has become a random storage area that must be navigated just to find the washer and dryer. Together, we will get "past the past" and make this a functional, organized space again.

How are you currently using this space? Folding laundry, feeding pets, hanging jackets, and storing bags? Everyone will greatly appreciate you taking the time to listen to their frustrations and their nonnegotiables for this space.

What are the top 5 knots that need untangling in this space? Not enough space to wash and fold clothes, tinker on projects, or charge handheld devices?

What activities would you like to do in this space? Efficiently do laundry, store handy household items, or store packages that need returning?

Check the condition of the space to determine if any repairs or structural/design changes need to be made. Place an X where you need to repair or reconsider your current setup. Go to chapter 6 for more details on what steps you can take here.

Doors:	__ Condition	__ Function
Shelves:	__ Condition	__ Function
Lighting:	__ Condition	__ Function
Style:	__ Condition	__ Function

Styles that make you smile. Unless you are hiring a British butler named Jeeves to run your household, you will spend a significant amount of time in this space. I suggest making it a style that will help you whistle while you work. I always loved Wonder Woman as a child, so that theme met my desire for fun and whimsical. I have displayed artwork from Etsy that shows Wonder Woman soaring through the night sky with a sign above her, "Keep calm and call Wonder Woman." The walls are painted Hot Tamale Red for my favorite candy.

I was cautioned about using such bright colors in a small space, but this is MY laundry room, and I followed my heart. Although I'm not typically a DIY paint person, we decided this area would be easy enough for my boys and me to foam roll the brown wooden cabinets white and install modern nickel handles.

We maximized the space by adding a floating shelf above the washer and dryer to house our four clean laundry baskets. Think about color-scheme combos that refresh your inner spirit and store those images electronically for future reference. I encourage you to make it a "happy place" to work in especially when you spend so much time doing "dirty" work in there.

Upper cupboards or shelving? Are your upper cabinets within arm's reach, or would installing additional shelves be more efficient? When standing in the space, what do you have to work with and what can be added? Are the shelves adjustable or fixed? Laundry cabinet depths tend to be shallow, which makes finding the right bin or basket for housing a variety of themes challenging. I often rotate baskets to sit horizontally to fit the space so be sure to measure the space accurately.

Here are some common laundry room items. Review this list and assess, based on your priorities, what needs to fit in your space.

- ✳ Back stock of food and beverages
- ✳ Back stock of school supplies
- ✳ Batteries
- ✳ Car care gear
- ✳ Clean and dirty cloths and towels
- ✳ Fabric cleaners: detergents, softeners, and stain removal
- ✳ Gifts and gift wrap-related items
- ✳ Cards
- ✳ Handheld vacuum
- ✳ Household handy tools
- ✳ Laundry baskets
- ✳ Lightbulbs
- ✳ Mystery pieces and parts
- ✳ Party supplies
- ✳ Paper goods
- ✳ Pet-related gear
- ✳ Picture hooks and nails
- ✳ Sewing gear
- ✳ Shoe cleaning materials
- ✳ Surface cleaners
- ✳ Tapes and glues

Errands and Returns

Ahhh, yes! Where do these go? Since this is the last chapter, it is going to go here! If an item is small, I tape the receipt to it and place it on top of my dryer and mark in my Brain Book the date I plan to drop it off and/or pick it up. If it is a large item, I tape the receipt to it and place it in a designated spot in the garage.

Keys, Keys, and More Keys! Installing a key rack in our home was literally … KEY. I resisted initially because I thought they were unsightly. Phil and Devon, then just two years old, convinced me otherwise. Devon would grab the keys from the counter and drop them into the trash. After purchasing multiple replacement keys, we installed the key rack, and it has worked well ever since.

ATTACK AND ASSIGN — COMBO PHASE

A laundry room is a core space that is used on a daily basis. You should keep in this area only the products and supplies you regularly need, use, or need to store. It all must serve a consistent purpose. Therefore, it makes sense from an efficiency standpoint to purge and place items into their respective categories during this combo phase. Then you can add/adjust shelving or alter the bins/basket size to accommodate storage for the variety of categories.

Laundry Guidelines

Guideline No. 1 – Decide your laundry schedule. Because I am the "want to get it done yesterday" type of girl, I start washing loads nonstop from Friday through Sunday night (during the off-peak energy hours) because that handles school clothes, soccer from the weekend, and cleaning towels. Monday is put away day. Tuesday is for towels, and every other week the sheets get changed. Maybe you prefer doing a little laundry every day. Devise a game plan that works for you.

Guideline No. 2 – Your *dirty* clothes hamper needs to be separate from your *clean* clothes basket. A dirty clothes hamper must be hearty in structure, not floppy or woven (which can snag clothing). Phil and I have a double hamper in our master bathroom which offers two sections—one for light clothes and one for darks.

My boys share a room and share one tall mesh hamper on wheels. It doubles as a basketball hoop for them to toss in clothes and dunking small rubber balls when the urge arises … which is daily … such is the life of having boys! For clients with multi-level homes, most prefer having one central hamper location in the hallway instead of multiple ones located in multiple bedrooms.

Guideline No. 3 – Start using my magical mesh bag laundry system. If I were to be remembered decades from now in the Organizing History Hall of Fame (if there isn't one, there should be), I want to be most noted for this solution.

When Devon was born and constantly filling diapers, I never encountered so many loads of laundry in my life. I was driven to devise a more productive method. The teeny tiny baby socks spread everywhere like confetti at a party I did not want to attend. I had to corral them, so I bought Whitmor®, zippered mesh bags for washing lingerie. A large and a small sack came in one package for only about $8. It was a perfect way to keep Devon's socks in one place during the wash. The inner organizing nerd in me seriously flipped out that day. You have no idea my state of utter enlightenment. I wasn't even a professional organizer yet with clients. I was just creating systems and finding solutions to everyday problems.

I immediately (like that day or the next) purchased more sacks because I realized that one mesh sack could be binder-clipped and hanging open on Devon's dirty clothes hamper and that I would need extras. I think at least four sacks per family is a good starting place.

Identify each family member with a colored ribbon. Eventually, Phil and I joined the party. To differentiate *our* sets from *Devon's*, we knotted ribbons through the zipper holes. Devon's was green, mine red and white polka dots, and Phil's was black. When Oliver joined the family, his ribbon had doggie prints on them. We clipped ours to opposite sides of our dirty clothes' hamper.

For adults only. My sack is used to corral my socks, undies, and bras (be sure to hook the straps together to avoid the hooks getting tangled in the mesh bag). Phil uses his for dress and athletic socks.

For kiddos only. Refer to the Laundry Chapter in my *Ignite the Organizer In Your Child* book on how to empower (and not enable) kids when it comes to laundry. My boys put away their laundry in the most efficient manner possible. The mesh sack system is even incorporated in their sport bags. Game changer forever people!

Don't overstuff your bag. Fill your bag about 60 percent of the way, so its contents have enough room to move around, get properly washed, and dried thoroughly. Once filled, zip the bag up and toss it into the hamper to hang with the other dirty clothes. Then, immediately grab a new empty sack waiting for you at the hamper bottom, binder clip it to the edge of your hamper, and open it for another round of filling to keep this magical method moving.

Guideline No. 4 – Stains are a pain, but Dreft is the best. Back when diaper blow outs were all the rage during my new adventure as a mother ... Dreft® baby detergent was suggested for washing Devon's newborn baby clothes. It was a bit pricey for detergent, but it really got the job done like no other product I had tried. I honestly can't recall the exact moment I realized Dreft could offer my laundry life something far more, but at some point, I ventured off and tried using it solely as a *stain remover.*

I probably had run out of my other products and wanted to simplify my product purchases or save money. I soaked a stain spot with Dreft and then used an old tooth brush to gently rub it further into the clothing fibers. I then placed the item in a kitchen mixing bowl, filled the bowl with water until the entire item was submerged, and let it all soak overnight. I pulled the item out sparkling new and stain free, like the incident had never happened. Dreft is not only good for diaper blowouts, it dissolves food, dirt, and even red wine on white linen placemats. Laundering at my house is like a Vegas magic show!

Have Dreft, will travel. Like an American Express Card, "I never leave home without my Dreft!" I love this stuff so much that I take a small travel bottle of it on every trip. It has saved my family from ruining our most favorite clothing while traveling because we can let the item soak overnight in the hotel sink.

As my boys got older, I bravely started wearing white again; however, my hormones had kicked up a notch causing nasty grey armpit stains, which for a soccer mom is soooo not a good look! No fear for the Laundress Stain Solution System® was near! Their products are off the charts amazing for whites. Like the future of your whites is sooo bright you gotta wear shades … for reals! I love their eco-friendly product line and sophisticated branding that makes doing laundry feel fancy!

Guideline No. 5 – Decide what to hang dry and where. In our home, all tops are pulled from the washer and hung to dry directly on their respective hangers. We only use white tubular, gray slimline or crystal-clip hangers (some nicer athletic bottoms, skirts, or pants may hang dry).

I use an InterMetro® chrome laundry cart to hang dry clothing. Each family member's hanging section is labeled and divided using Xangar® foam dividers, so filing and retrieving everyone's clothes is obvious. Since our laundry cart is in the garage, I joke how our "clothes dry like bacon" so quickly on the cart in our dry Arizona heat.

I have yet to see one curious critter on our clothes or see the clothing become dusty when hung in the garage. If you regard your garage space as equally important as your interior space, then it will make all the difference. However, if space permits, add a cart in your laundry room on the end of both machines or install a permanent rod that does not hinder your work space or your access to either the washer or dryer.

Guideline No. 6 – Decide what to dry in the dryer. The rest of our bottoms are tossed in the dryer. From jammies to jeans to athletic shorts and, of course, all our family's magical mesh sacks!

Guideline No. 7 – Laundry basket intervention. I am always surprised that people consistently purchase those massive plastic laundry baskets with holes on the sides. Is it so their clean clothes, small socks, and undies can easily stick out or fall through? Seriously, why? It makes absolutely no sense to me and never will. In addition, it takes triple the time to empty the massive thing, which is too awkward to hold, too bulky to store, and too big for a small person to carry.

For those who prefer folding and piling clean laundry on sofas or tables, this system will only be successful if you and/or your family are dedicated time management ninjas and immediately put it away. Otherwise, it creates more complications than resolutions, including family pets nestling on it, little ones knocking piles over, or family members failing to promptly put their items away. Efforts become wasted because the clean laundry is now sitting and getting dirty and dusty. Talk about a cycle of insanity!

Immediate laundry basket resolutions to implement:

Each family member needs his or her *own* individually labeled clean clothes laundry basket. For years, I have consistently used the Whitmor® brand soft woven strap basket with supportive wire construction. It is made in an array of colors and priced at $20. Why do I prefer this product rather than the traditional larger bulky white-holed plastic basket?

* **Takes under 15 minutes to empty.** The significantly smaller size makes it more manageable.

  Clever side handles. These are convenient for both little and big helping hands to pick up or slide for delivery.

* **Avoids the "folding step" all together.** Clean clothes from the dryer are just tossed into that family members basket and then, depending on the item, can be placed directly in their drawer.

* **Easily stores four across on a floating shelf above your washer and dryer,** which frees up valuable surface space so you can work faster and more efficiently.

* **The tightly woven pattern allows each basket to duel function as a "catch all."** For instance, upon returning from the drug store to buy toothpaste, I remove my visor, recycle the toothpaste box in the kitchen, and place both items in my personally labeled clean laundry basket, instead of on the kitchen counter to deal with "later." When I deliver clean clothes to my bedroom, the visor is returned to its labeled shelf and the toothpaste to my bathroom drawer. Beyond smart and efficient!

* **Label your basket with one of our clever organizing tags.** Ranging from a chevron pattern to cheery multiple stripes, these labels will soon be offered on our website. Labels ensure that every family members' basket is properly identified and can then be placed in the same consistent spot in the laundry room. Once empty, it is ready to be filled and returned for the next laundry round.

Guideline No. 8 – Transfer items from the dryer to each family member's basket. We literally just chuck it all in the basket. Once ready for bedroom delivery, the basket is pulled off the floating shelf, placed on the floor, and the dried hanger items are folded in half on top. Time for that family member to get going on delivery.

Guideline No. 9 – Hang all hanger themed items for each family member in their labeled section. Shazam! Since the labeling does the speaking for you, all family members can easily locate their hangered clothes and properly return them to their closet. This transfer can be handled in one move and completed within minutes.

Guideline No. 10 – Place folded themed items in rainbow order on their respective shelves or in a drawer. Remember to position the item *bookend style with the finished edge up* so clothes can be viewed in one glance, instead of just seeing what lies on the top of the stack. I find this especially helpful for athletic clothing. The tops of your drawer sections should be nicely labeled to guide you along the way!

Guideline No. 11 – Return laundry basket to its proper position in the laundry room. It's now ready to go again. If one family member is overwhelmed after a rough day, it's always a nice gesture to empty their basket for them … we are all a family and *all* need to support one another.

Supplies

Let's circle back to my lovely list of laundry room themes. By now, you have already measured and gathered up some containers from your Bin of Bins to start sorting your nonnegotiables for the room.

Place and position items according to priority. Review the list of supplies from earlier in the chapter and number the items according to priority. Then, place the more commonly used items on lower shelves and less commonly used items in upper locations.

Review and reconsider themes. Do you need your lightbulbs in your laundry room, or could they be stored elsewhere? Do you have duplicate tape measures or hammers? It might be nice to have that spare set inside on a lower shelf.

Simplify your party supplies. I only buy clear plastic utensils so they can go with any type of festive event. I also find it more versatile to purchase solid colored plates rather than patterned ones. I complement these basics by purchasing festive napkins, whether for birthdays or holidays. Any leftover napkins are used at family dinners to remind us of the recent celebration.

ACCOUNTABLE PHASE

Unless you plan on joining a nearby nudist colony, you need to stay on top of getting your laundry done as promptly as possible. This needs to be a weekly priority in your life.

I thought it would be helpful to share some of my own lifestyle systems that *reduce* my laundry load, while increasing my productivity:

Lifestyle Tip No. 1 – Select one pajama set for the week. Phil and I put our PJ sets in our nightstand drawers and swap them out at the end of the week. My boys store their sets under the pillow on their bed—one set for the week. Easy to remember and rotate.

Lifestyle Tip No. 2 – Select one bath and face towel for the week and use one hand towel per day. Just like the jammies, use and promptly hang your towels for the week. If you are a sweaty person or workout often (like my hubby), then you may need to swap out once midweek. I like to change the hand towels almost every other day to keep germs at bay.

Lifestyle Tip No. 3 – Adopt the mesh sack system for travel. Talk about scoring big on a laundry and efficiency for multiple family members. Traveling with mesh sacks makes laundry time on the return trip go so much faster.

Linen Logarithms

I would say 100 percent of our clients' families have amazing storage for some type of linen closet, but it is gravely overstocked and, therefore, underutilized. To solve this space dilemma and effectively manage the linen closet, you need only to follow this basic math formula.

<u>Linen Logarithm:</u>

(3) Bath + (3) Hand + (1) Face Towel / Per Family Member

Example:

Total Family of 4 Linen Logarithm = 12 Bath + 12 Hand + 4 Face

Bath and hand towels are trifolded so only one clean folded edge (not multiple side edges) shows when stored under each bathroom sink. Face towels are folded in half (not in quarters), so they lay flat nicely next to the other towels.

Bed Sheet Sets: 2 Per Bed = (1) on the Bed + (1) Stored. Fold your fitted sheet, then your flat and one pillow case. Stack all pieces together. Take the matching pillow case and place the bed sheet set inside, wrapping the case around the set like a taco.

Place on your linen shelf with the folded edge facing you. It's so easy to put away and retrieve in one shot. BAM! Even if you mix/match sheet set patterns, still create complete bed sets. Donate any excessive extras accordingly.

Pool Towels: (1) Per Family Member + (2) Extras for Guests. Guests may forget their pool towels, so it is nice to have a few to provide for them. When hosting an event remind people to bring their own. Store pool towels in the bathroom or storage closet closest to the pool area. Install hooks on a nearby wall to keep your pool area organized or simply hang an over-the-door towel rack on your pool fence.

What about linens for my guests? Guests will use your extra fresh towels and an appropriate bed linen set. What if you don't think your towels/linens are not nice enough for guests? Well then, frankly, you shouldn't be using them either! Promptly upgrade your old rag towels/linens and donate what remains in that stock. If your linens are still "not acceptable" for your guests, then there is a place called "a hotel" where they are more than welcome to stay.

Here's to more love and less work during laundry time!

You have earned another bundle of kindling to keep your organizing flame burning within if you successfully completed the following:

Assess Phase

❏ You have assessed the floor, lights, doors, cabinets, shelves, electrical outlets, and working surface of your laundry space.

❏ Pictures were taken of the space, and you feel confident moving forward.

❏ You have identified your personal style vibe for the space.

❏ Cabinets have been reviewed for condition and measured for future solutions.

❏ A specific location has been designated for both small and large returns and errands.

❏ The common Laundry Room Supply List has been reviewed, assessed, and ranked based on your priorities and potential space.

❏ Your storage system has been identified and agreed upon with all family members.

Attack Phase and Assign Phase

❏ You have developed a laundry schedule and system for moving dirty items to the laundry room and clean items back to their space.

❑ All Laundry Room items have been labeled and placed in position according to priority.

Accountable Phase

❑ You have considered and/or adopted one or more of the lifestyle suggestions.
❑ You have applied the Linen Logarithms to your household.

MATTERS

— OF —

REFERENCE

14

THE COACHING CORNER: A FEW QUICK WINS TO CONQUER ANYTIME

How do you eat a warm, gooey glazed donut? One delicious bite at a time! How do you untangle years of compiling collections? One shelf at a time!

I totally get you! Putting your heart, head, and hands together is not meant to be a daunting process, and I didn't design the book to make you feel overwhelmed and frozen in frustration. No thank you!

If you are feeling inspired to take ANY action at all while reading this book (or need to take a break between chapters), I've created a few quick-win projects that can be completed in a very, very short amount of time!

They are designed to allow you to be creative and to help you crank out simple, yet productive work to proudly brag about on social media (maybe you'll inspire others to follow suit). We would LOVE to do the happy dance right along WITH YOU!

Time to turn up the tunes! Reference this Coaching Corner ANY time you need a confidence boost or if you just need my help!

Let's Get Your Heart Right

The deeper we examine ourselves, the better we can define and organize the life we want. When we turn the spotlight off products and direct it inward, we will gravitate toward healthier, clutter-free lives.

Organizing products are wonderful and give us solutions with style and vision—but that is only one part of the organizing process. It can be physically and mentally exhausting, but your inner organizer has been ignited and you know that following the steps, in proper order, is the only way the process works.

Moving forward, review the list of "Whys" that you checked in the introduction. Share them with someone who supports your efforts to become more organized. Your unique list of whys is what will persuade your head and heart, so your hands can make it happen.

Are you ready to commit to this new way of feeling?
_____ *Yes, I am!*

Let's Get Your Head Right

Everyone, everywhere around the world, juggles and struggles with daily challenges. Just like you, they are trying to raise a family, care for a loved one, have a successful career, and keep a well-ordered home. If you have family members (furry friends, too) with any special needs, the challenges escalate.

Are you ready to commit to this new way of thinking?
___ *Yes, I am!*

Let's Get Your Hands Right

Let's dial back expectations and anxieties, and turn up your confidence with an easy, Three-Wins-in-Three-Days Challenge using your Organizing Tool Kit:

Quick Win #1 – Clean out your bag in 15 minutes

1. Empty your purse or bag onto a clean table.
2. Wipe it down with a baby wipe or cleaning cloth.
3. Toss the trash, recycle the recycling.
4. Clip together receipts and business cards that can be processed later.
5. Secure tech-related gear with a rubber band.
6. Gather snacks, mints, and meds together.
7. Relocate unnecessary items to your car, desk, office, or elsewhere.
8. Add any essentials that you are missing.
9. Smile wide about what you just accomplished!

Quick Win #2 – Clean out your car in 30 minutes

1. Empty the front of your car.
2. Grab four cookie sheets or boxes to separate money, snacks, and tech supplies.

3. Add any missing supplies.

4. Repeat steps 1-3 for back seat and trunk. Maybe add a box, basket, or tote to secure groceries or sports items when transporting them.

5. Use a lint brush or vacuum to clean.

6. Pat yourself on the back for a challenge well done!

Quick Win #3 – Create a passwords book in 60 minutes

1. Quickly tape or staple all personal password snippets onto an 8x11 inch paper in rough alphabetical order (A's together, B's together, and so on.)

2. Collect passwords from family members.

3. Put the passwords page into protective sleeve for easy reference.

4. Add page to existing passwords book or spreadsheet when time permits.

5. Or, if you prefer digital, investigate numerous password applications.

6. Use one book for professional/business contacts and one for family.

7. Use only one master system for your family.

Final Thoughts

Have you referred to this chapter frequently? Are you still having difficulty completing the three organizing challenges? Here are next steps to help:

Reach out to us directly through the contact form at **WurthOrganizing.com** and schedule a complimentary consultation or future coaching session. We will celebrate victories and overcome challenges together. You are no longer in this alone, because you will be able to lean on me until you are able to stand stronger on your own.

Like we always say …

Happy Days Come Through Organized Ways!

RESOURCE GUIDE

All of the following printables and products referenced in this book can be found under the Shop tab at:

WurthOrganizing.com

Ignite Your Organizing Personality

- ❏ Banker Box
- ❏ Brother PT – 1890 Label Maker

Kicking Ace: Mastering the Four A's of Organizing

- ❏ Photo and File Sharing App: Dropbox
- ❏ Quattro Stagioni Spice Jars
- ❏ InteriorDesign Linus Trays
- ❏ Like-It Brand Bricks Solution
- ❏ OXO Good Grips POP Canister Set
- ❏ Hermetic Glass Storage Jars
- ❏ Anchor Hocking Glass Containers

Closets & Bedrooms

- ❏ Apps for Private Postings: OfferUp and LetGo
- ❏ Joy Mangano Hangers
- ❏ My 100 Item: Wardrobe Wonderlist
- ❏ Clothing Theme Tag Printable
- ❏ Elfa, Avera, and Laren Closet Solutions

Shove Out the Shame and Drive in Your Car

- ❏ Geared Up Garage Checklist
- ❏ Garage Sale and Private Posting Printable
- ❏ Blue Hawk 5-Tier Shelving Unit
- ❏ InterMetro Shelving
- ❏ Elfa Shelving & Utility Boards
- ❏ Sterilite Totes: Weathertight & Stacker
- ❏ Gladiator GearTracks & GearWall Panels
- ❏ Iris Store-It-All Trunk
- ❏ Black + Decker Pivoting Cordless Hand Vacuum

Killing the Paperwork Virus

- ❏ Office Organizing Checklist: Home
- ❏ Office Organizing Checklist: Business
- ❏ Weekly Desk Planner - Exacompta: Space 24
- ❏ Leuchtturm1917 Pen Loop
- ❏ Email Management App: UnrollMe.com

Creating an Office of Orderly Ways

- ❏ Office Organizing Checklist: Home
- ❏ Office Organizing Checklist: Business
- ❏ 3M Command Hooks
- ❏ Nite Ize™ Tech Cords
- ❏ Native Union Charging Cable and Key Chain
- ❏ Elfa Solutions
- ❏ Ikea Lack Wall Shelf
- ❏ Magnolia Product Line

Hobby Zones

- ❑ Daily Audio Bible App
- ❑ Poppin Office Accessories
- ❑ Like-It Modular Drawers

Making Meals No Big Deal

- ❑ Kitchen Themed Printable List
- ❑ Cutco Homemakers Knife Set
- ❑ Architec Original Gripper Cutting Board
- ❑ Ball (Bernardin) Plastic Freezer Jars
- ❑ Crate & Barrel Clear Bowl Lid Set of 12
- ❑ Pyrex Simply Store Glass Round Set
- ❑ Cambro Commercial Food Safe Containers
- ❑ Bamboo Expandable Utensil Tray
- ❑ Mega Expand a Shelf 3-Tier
- ❑ OXO Good Grips POP Canister Set

Laundry Room La La Land

- ❑ Whitmor Laundry Mesh Bags
- ❑ Dreft Newborn Liquid Detergent
- ❑ Laundress Laundry and Fabric Care
- ❑ InterMetro Chrome Laundry Cart
- ❑ Xangar Closet Spacers
- ❑ Organizing Tag Collection: WurthOrganizing.com
- ❑ Whimor Woven Strap Basket

A THOUSAND THANKS

No, really! Thank you for your kind investment in purchasing this book and all the time you devoted to reading it. It came directly from my heart in the hopes of immediately moving yours. Please share freely with others.

I would love to hear how the teaching and organizing methods you learned have impacted you! Your feedback not only helps make improvements for future books but also pays it forward by impacting many readers not yet found.

You can stay find out about upcoming books, events, and workshops by registering for my monthly **Teachable Tips Newsletter** via my website: **WurthOrganizing.com**.

It would make my day glow brighter if you would snap a shot of yourself with the book using **#ignitetheorganizerinyou** and share what you learned on any of our social sites. To find us on social media, search for Wurth Organizing on your favorite social media and follow us to get great organizing tips and suggestions. By staying connected, we can keep your inner fire burning bright and together we can ignite the hearts and heal the homes of hundreds more!

Happy Days Come Through Organized Ways!

ACKNOWLEDGEMENTS

To my writing and editing coach Rose, I will forever be grateful to you for taking this journey with me over the past two and a half years. Your excitement for this book never ceased, and taught me to be a better writer along the way. To my agent Tess, who believed in me before my company and vision even developed. You have been such a supportive role model and friend who continued to look out for my best interests. To my dear friend Valerie, who has walked and talked me through endless changes (and ledges) as a fellow mompreneur. I cherish you and your confident wisdom so very much. To my dear friend Kristin, who has helped promote my business and never doubted what I could accomplish. To my sister friend Abbie, your loving friendship is a rare gem to me and an emotional support like no other. To my Stroller Strides gals—Sonja, Ali, Missy, Michelle, Shira, Patrice, Jean, and Leah—the driving forces who convinced me to start my business over 12 years ago and never stopped celebrating with me along the way. To my amazing team manager Tifanny, you are the rock when I need a solid foundation and the roll when we need to change direction for business growth or for this book. To my organizing crew of gurus—Kiera, Aimee, Trish, Grace, Katie, and Sheri—your encouragement and support has pushed me forward when I felt like I was standing still. Lastly, thank you to Joe for writing my foreword and supporting my mission to heal others. You are a man of so many talents, and I am grateful for not only the privilege of working with you, but personally knowing you and continually inspired by you and those you impact every day forth.

ABOUT THE AUTHOR

DANIELLE WURTH is the founder and CEO of Wurth Organizing as well as a professional organizer, speaker, author, and self-proclaimed recovering perfectionist. Since 2007, she and her team of organizing gurus have used her psychology-based approach to transform the lives of over one thousand individuals, families, and businesses. Her mindful and easy-to-implement organizing methods teach the benefits of living a healthy, intentional, and organized lifestyle.

Danielle's sole purpose and the inspiration for her work involve guiding clients to thrive and to reach their absolute best potential in their home and personal life. All too often, she has found clients were focusing on fancy solutions before examining their habits and their actual needs. She helps them to understand *why* past methods and solutions have failed and teaches them *what* to do to overcome frustrations and lead the happier, healthier home and personal life they always craved.

She is honored to be the only Official Brand Partner for the Container Store in Metro Phoenix with work featured in *HGTV Magazine*, *Real Simple* magazine, *The List* television show, former columnist for *InRecovery* magazine, and a contributor to Fox 10 News and Channel 3 *Good Morning Arizona*. Danielle is the author of *Ignite the Organizer in Your Child*, the companion organizing book for parents and school-aged kids.

She lives in Scottsdale, Arizona, with her handsome hubby and her two soccer loving sons. You will find her embracing her inner soccer mom at every game, cheering them on!

Your life is … Wurth investing in.

Your life is … Wurth embracing today.

Your life is … Wurth Organizing!

WurthOrganizing.com

Printed in November 2021
by Rotomail Italia S.p.A., Vignate (MI) - Italy